SPECTRUM

Geometry

Grade 5

Spectrum®
An imprint of Carson-Dellosa Publishing LLC
P.O. Box 35665
Greensboro, NC 27425 USA

© 2014 Carson-Dellosa Publishing LLC. Except as permitted under the United States Copyright Act, no part of this publication may be reproduced, stored, or distributed in any form or by any means (mechanically, electronically, recording, etc.) without the prior written consent of Carson-Dellosa Publishing LLC. Spectrum® is an imprint of Carson-Dellosa Publishing LLC.

Printed in the USA • All rights reserved.   ISBN 978-1-4838-0479-8

03-068151151

Table of Contents — Grade 5

Introduction 4

Chapter 1 Points, Lines, Rays, and Angles
Chapter 1 Pretest 5
Practice Pages 6–13
Chapter 1 Posttest 14

Chapter 2 Problem Solving: Points, Lines, Rays, and Angles
Chapter 2 Pretest 15
Practice Pages 16–21
Chapter 2 Posttest 22

Chapter 3 Geometric Figures
Chapter 3 Pretest 23
Practice Pages 24–30
Chapter 3 Posttest 31

Chapter 4 Problem Solving: Geometric Figures
Chapter 4 Pretest 32
Practice Pages 33–37
Chapter 4 Posttest 38

Mid-Test Chapters 1–4 39–40

Chapter 5 Perimeter, Area, and Volume
Chapter 5 Pretest 41
Practice Pages 42–52
Chapter 5 Posttest 53

Chapter 6 Problem Solving: Perimeter, Area, and Volume
Chapter 6 Pretest 54
Practice Pages 55–62
Chapter 6 Posttest 63

Chapter 7 The Coordinate Plane
Chapter 7 Pretest 64
Practice Pages 65–75
Chapter 7 Posttest 76

Final Test Chapters 1–7 77–82

Scoring Record for Pretests, Posttests, Mid-Test, and Final Test 83

Answer Key 84–96

Introduction — Grade 5

Spectrum Geometry is designed to build a solid foundation in geometry for your fifth grader. Aligned to the fifth grade Common Core State Standards for geometry, every page equips your child with the confidence to master geometry. Helpful examples provide step-by-step guidance to teach new concepts, followed by a variety of practice pages that will sharpen your child's skills and efficiency at problem solving. Use the Pretests, Posttests, Mid-Test, and Final Test as the perfect way to track your child's progress and identify where he or she needs extra practice.

Common Core State Standards Alignment: Geometry Grade 5

Domain: Measurement and Data	
Standard	Aligned Practice Pages
5.MD.3a	50, 54, 63
5.MD.3b	50, 54, 63
5.MD.4	50, 54, 63
5.MD.5a	41, 48–53, 54, 59–63, 77, 79–80, 82
5.MD.5b	41, 48–53, 54, 59–63, 77, 79–80, 82
5.MD.5c	50, 54, 63

Domain: Geometry	
Standard	Aligned Practice Pages
5.G.1	64–76, 78
5.G.2	64–76, 78
5.G.3	23, 26–27, 78
5.G.4	23–28, 31, 32, 34–38, 40, 78

* © Copyright 2010. National Governors Association Center for Best Practices and Council of Chief State School Officers. All rights reserved.

Check What You Know

Points, Lines, Rays, and Angles

Use a protractor to measure each angle.

a   **b**

1.

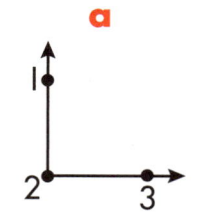   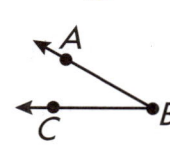

∠ = _____ = _____ °   ∠ = _____ = _____ °

Identify each pair of lines as parallel, perpendicular, or intersecting.

2.

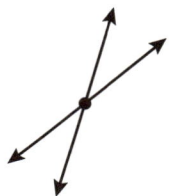   

_____   _____

3.

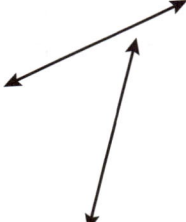   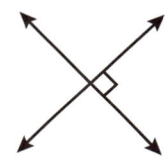

_____   _____

Name each angle. Label as acute, obtuse, or right.

4.

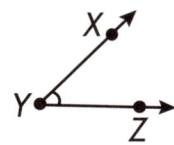   _____   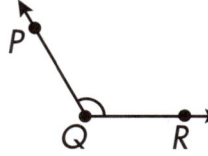   _____

_____   _____

5.

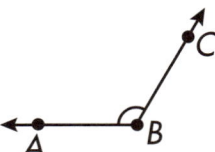   _____   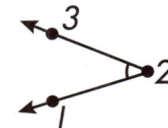   _____

_____   _____

Spectrum Geometry
Grade 5

Chapter 1
Points, Lines, Rays, and Angles

Points, Lines, and Rays

SCORE ___/12

 A **point** can be represented by a dot. The point on the left is called point *A*.

 A **line** passes through two points. The line *AB* (denoted $\overleftrightarrow{AB}$) is the line that passes through points *A* and *B*. Also, $\overleftrightarrow{AB} = \overleftrightarrow{BA}$.

 A **line segment** starts at a point *A* and ends at a point *B*, and includes all points in between. The segment *AB* (denoted $\overline{AB}$) is the same as $\overline{BA}$.

 A **ray** is a straight line that begins at an endpoint (*A*) and goes on forever in a certain direction. The ray on the left is written as $\overrightarrow{AB}$.

Identify the following as point, line, line segment, or ray. Then, name each figure.

1.  _____    _____

   _____   _____

2.    _____   • R _____

   _____   _____

3. ←•G——•H→   _____   •P ↘•Q _____

   _____   _____

Spectrum Geometry
Grade 5

NAME _____

SCORE ☐ / 13

Points, Lines, and Rays

Identify the following figures.

a	b	c	d

1.

   _____   _____   _____   _____

Complete the figures.

2. _____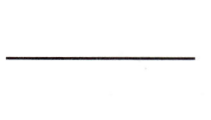

      line   ray   line segment   vertex

Draw these figures.

3. line segment

   ray

   vertex

   point

   line

Spectrum Geometry
Grade 5

Chapter 1
Points, Lines, Rays, and Angles

Points, Lines, and Rays

Draw and name the following figures. The first one has been done for you.

1. line AB

2. ray FG

3. line JK

4. line segment MN

5. ray QP

6. line segment CD

7. ray GF

8. line segment JK

Angles

The **angle** ABC (denoted ∠ABC) is made of ray BA ($\vec{BA}$) and ray BC ($\vec{BC}$). The point where the two rays intersect is called the **vertex**. The vertex of ∠ABC is point B.

Identify the rays and vertex of each angle. Name the angle.

1.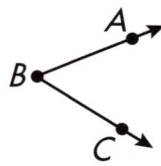

rays: _____

_____

vertex: _____

angle: _____

2.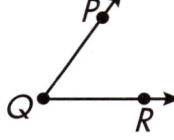

rays: _____

_____

vertex: _____

angle: _____

3.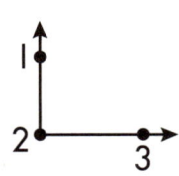

rays: _____

_____

vertex: _____

angle: _____

4.

rays: _____

_____

vertex: _____

angle: _____

Spectrum Geometry
Grade 5

Measuring Angles

A **protractor** is used to measure an angle. The angle is measured in degrees.

A **right angle** measures exactly 90°.

An **acute angle** measures less than 90°.

An **obtuse angle** measures greater than 90° but less than 180°.

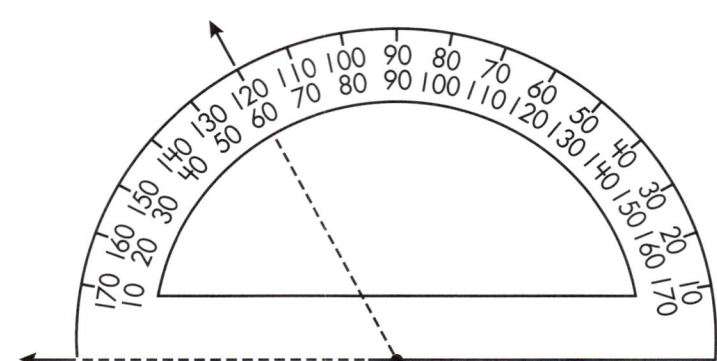

Identify each angle as right, acute, or obtuse.

	a	Type of Angle	b	Type of Angle
1.		_____	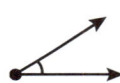	_____
2.		_____		_____
3.	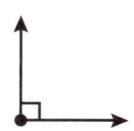	_____		_____

Measuring Angles

Name each angle. Write whether it is acute (A), right (R), or obtuse (O). Then, measure the angle.

1. a b

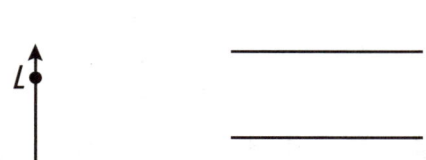 _____ 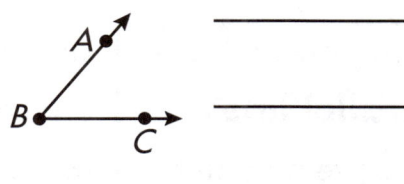 _____

_____   _____

_____   _____

2.

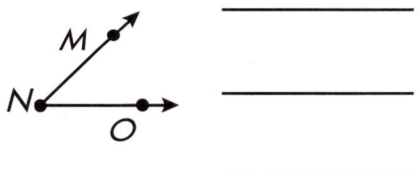 _____ 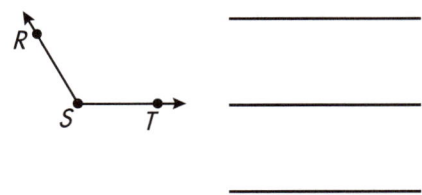 _____

_____   _____

_____   _____

3.

  _____ 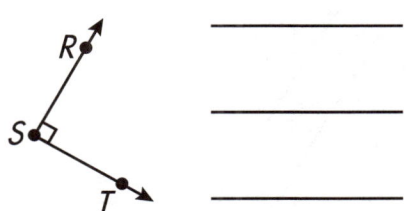 _____

_____   _____

_____   _____

Spectrum Geometry
Grade 5

NAME _____

Parallel and Perpendicular Lines

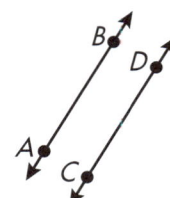 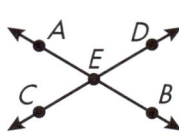 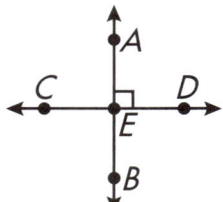

Lines like $\overleftrightarrow{AB}$ and $\overleftrightarrow{CD}$ are called **parallel lines** since they have no points in common. $\overleftrightarrow{AB}$ and $\overleftrightarrow{CD}$ will never intersect.

Lines like $\overleftrightarrow{AB}$ and $\overleftrightarrow{CD}$ are called **intersecting lines**. They have one point in common, point E. $\overleftrightarrow{AB}$ intersects $\overleftrightarrow{CD}$ at point E.

Lines like $\overleftrightarrow{AB}$ and $\overleftrightarrow{CD}$ are called **perpendicular lines**. They form a right angle, shown by the symbol ⌐ in the angle.

Identify each pair of lines as parallel, intersecting, or perpendicular.

	a	Type of Lines	b	Type of Lines
1.	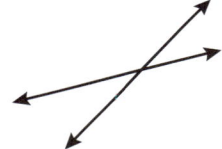	_____	↔ ↔	_____
2.	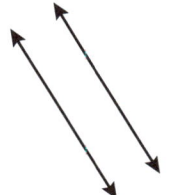	_____	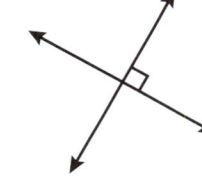	_____
3.	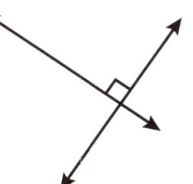	_____	↔ ⟋	_____

Spectrum Geometry
Grade 5

Chapter 1
Points, Lines, Rays, and Angles

Parallel and Perpendicular Lines

Identify each pair of lines as parallel, perpendicular, or intersecting.

	a	b	c
1.	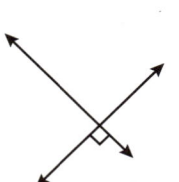	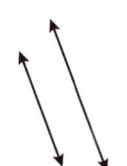	
2.	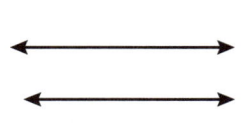		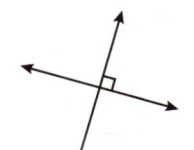
3.	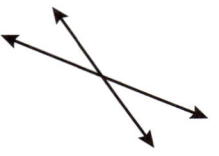	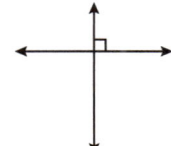	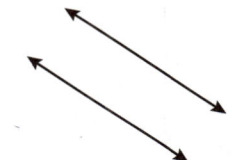
4.	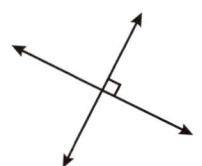	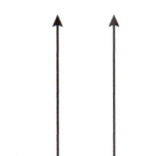	

NAME _____

Check What You Learned

Points, Lines, Rays, and Angles

Identify these geometric figures: point, line, line segment, ray, and vertex.

           a   **b**

1. _____   _____

2. _____   _____

Identify each pair of lines as parallel, intersecting, or perpendicular.

3. _____   _____

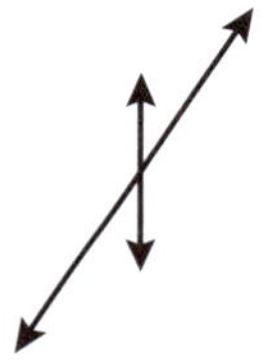

4. _____   _____

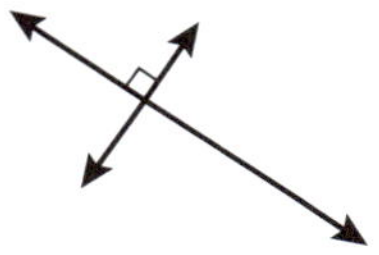

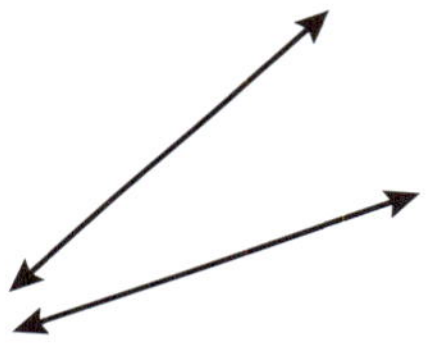

Name each angle. Label as acute, obtuse, or right.

5. _____   _____

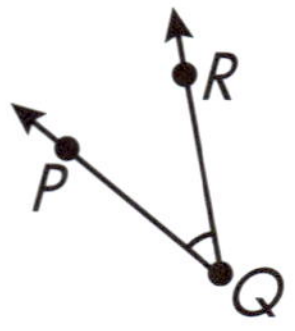

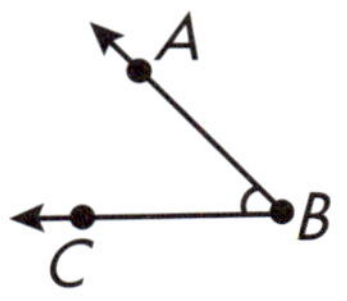

6. _____   _____

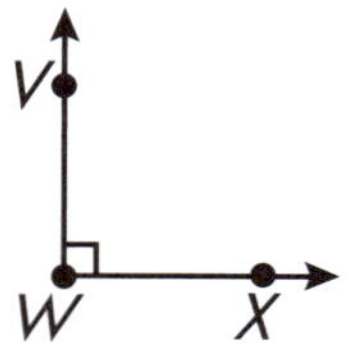

Spectrum Geometry
Grade 5

Check What You Know

Problem Solving: Points, Lines, Rays, and Angles

Read the problem carefully and solve. Show your work under each question.

Park planners make plans for small and large parks. Often, the final plans are quite complex. However, even complex plans are made of simple parts. Students at Marshall School look carefully at some park plans to find the simpler parts.

1. Joanne looks at this diagram. Does the diagram show a line or a line segment? What is the name of the figure?

   _____

2. In one of the park plans, Chris finds an angle like the one shown below. Name the angle. Is the angle acute, obtuse, or right?

   _____

3. Sheila finds the lines below in the plans. Is this pair of lines parallel, perpendicular, or intersecting?

   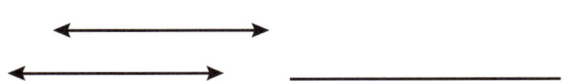
   _____

4. Matt measures the angle below. Use a protractor to measure the angle and record the number.

   _____

Spectrum Geometry
Grade 5

Chapter 2
Problem Solving: Points, Lines, Rays, and Angles

NAME _____

SCORE ⬤/3

Points, Lines, Rays, and Angles

Read the problem carefully and solve. Show your work under each question.

Mr. Spencer's math class studies the use of symbols in math. Right now, the students are studying symbols used in geometry. Mr. Spencer shows examples of how the symbols are used. He asks the students to draw diagrams that are like his examples.

1. Helga draws line segment $\overline{AB}$. Draw and label a line segment $\overline{CD}$ in the space below.

2. Ellis describes ray $\overrightarrow{AB}$ shown below. He says the ray starts at point A, passes through B, and extends forever. Draw and label a ray $\overrightarrow{EF}$ in the space below.

3. Terry sees that line $\overleftrightarrow{AB}$ passes through points A and B. This line is shown below. In the space below, draw and label the line $\overleftrightarrow{KL}$.

Spectrum Geometry
Grade 5

NAME _____

SCORE ▢ / 8

Points, Lines, Rays, and Angles

> **Helpful Hint**
>
> The symbol for a **point** is a dot.
>
> A **line** passes through two points.
>
> An **angle** is made of two rays starting from the same point.
>
> The point where the two rays connect is called the **vertex**.

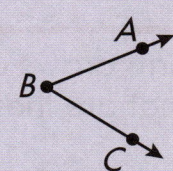

4. Ariel draws an angle shown below on the board. She labels the angle. Name the rays, the vertex, and the angle.

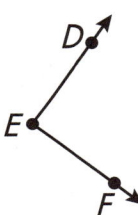

Rays: _____ and _____

Vertex: _____

Angle: _____

5. Joan draws the angle shown below on her paper. Name the angle, rays, and the vertex.

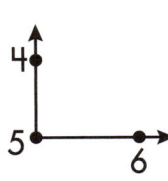

Angle: _____

Rays: _____ and _____

Vertex: _____

Spectrum Geometry
Grade 5

Chapter 2
Problem Solving: Points, Lines, Rays, and Angles

17

NAME _____

SCORE ◯/3

Parallel and Perpendicular Lines

Read the problem carefully and solve. Show your work under each question.

Ms. Tsai's social studies class studies geography. Students study how mapmakers create maps. Students draw street maps of their neighborhoods as an assignment.

1. Norm draws a section of a street that looks like the lines shown in the diagram. What are these lines called?

_____ lines

2. Mia draws a diagram of two streets that cross like the lines shown below. What kind of lines are these?

_____ lines

3. Janet knows that the sides of her street are parallel. She labels two points on one side of the street J and L. She labels two points on the other side of the street F and H. Draw two parallel lines with these labels.

Spectrum Geometry
Grade 5

Parallel and Perpendicular Lines

> **Helpful Hint**
>
> **Parallel lines** never intersect.
>
> **Intersecting lines** touch at exactly one point.
>
> **Perpendicular lines** touch at exactly one point and form right angles.

4. Vicky draws a street corner that looks like the diagram below. What kind of lines are these?

_____ lines

5. Stan draws two lines that intersect but do not form right angles. The lines are $\overleftrightarrow{ST}$ and $\overleftrightarrow{UV}$. They cross at point R. Draw and label a diagram of the two lines.

Measuring Angles

Read the problem carefully and solve. Show your work under each question.

The Builtwell Home Design firm creates home plans for builders. Each home plan has many different angles. The students in a math class at Allendale School locate and name the angles on a set of blueprints.

1. Vanessa finds an angle at the edge of the roof that looks like the angle in the diagram below. What kind of angle is it?

    _____ angle

2. Kent sees an angle formed by the wall and floor. A picture of the angle is shown below. What is this angle called?

    _____ angle

3. Joseph identifies the angle at the peak of the roof. A picture of the angle is shown below. What kind of angle is this?

    _____ angle

Measuring Angles

> **Helpful Hint**
>
> A **protractor** is a tool used to measure angles.
>
> Angles are measured in degrees.
>
> A **right angle** measures exactly 90°.
>
> An **acute angle** measures less than 90°.
>
> An **obtuse angle** measures more than 90° but less than 180°.

4. Rosina measures the angle in the diagram below. This angle represents how two of the walls meet in the home plan. Use a protractor to measure and name the angle.

_____ _____

5. Mato looks at an angle in a plan for a railing on a deck. What is the measure of the angle? Using the labels, what is the name of this angle?

_____ _____

Check What You Learned

Problem Solving: Points, Lines, Rays, and Angles

Read the problem carefully and solve. Show your work under each question.

Kits for model boats have detailed directions. The directions have diagrams and written steps. The more complex models have more complex directions. Model boats have many lines and angles.

1. On the directions, Jordan looks at lines that look like the lines below. These lines appear to be what type of lines?

   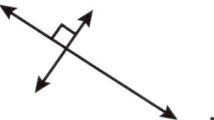 _____

2. On the front of the ship Bessie is building, there is an angle like the one in the diagram below. Name the angle. What kind of angle is this?

   _____ _____ angle

3. Ken measures the angle that the mast makes with the deck of a sailboat. Use a protractor and measure the angle below.

4. The masts of a sailboat are lines like the two shown below. What are these lines called?

   _____

NAME _____

Check What You Know

Geometric Figures

Identify the following quadrilaterals. Write the number that refers to the correct figure.

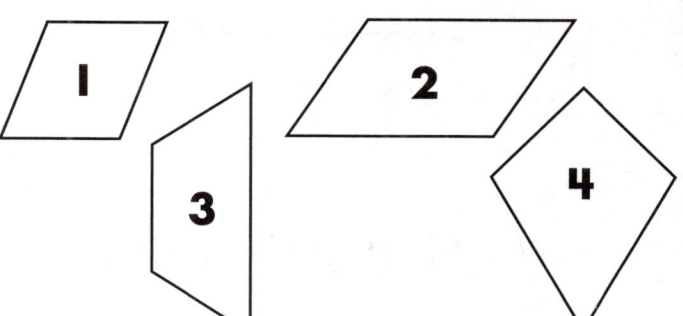

1. rhombus _____

2. kite _____

3. trapezoid _____

4. parallelogram _____

Identify the following polygons.

a Type

b Type

5.  _____   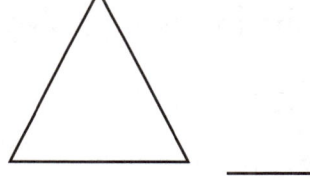 _____

6.  _____   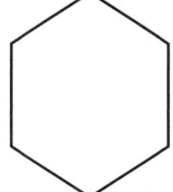 _____

Describe the surface of each solid figure.

7. 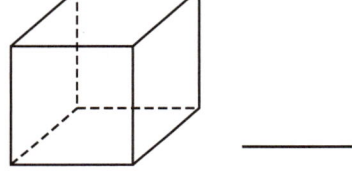 _____   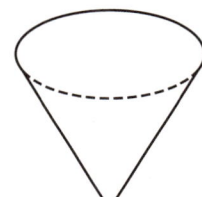 _____

Spectrum Geometry
Grade 5

Chapter 3
Geometric Figures

23

NAME _____

SCORE ☐ / 6

Polygons

A **polygon** is a closed shape that is formed by three or more sides. The name of a polygon is given by the number of sides the shape has.

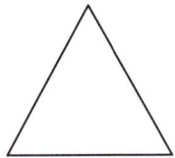 A triangle has 3 sides.   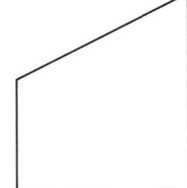 A quadrilateral has 4 sides.

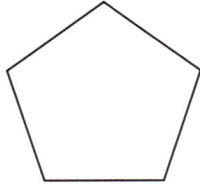 A pentagon has 5 sides.   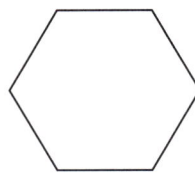 A hexagon has 6 sides.

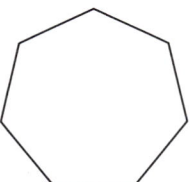 A heptagon has 7 sides.   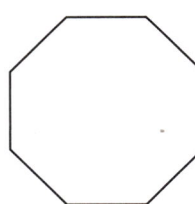 An octagon has 8 sides.

Identify each of the following polygons.

	a	Type	**b**	Type

1. 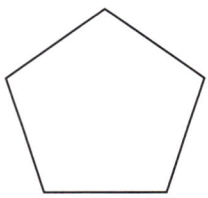 _____   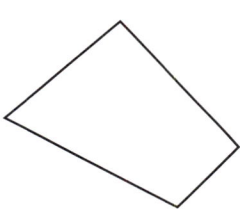 _____

2. 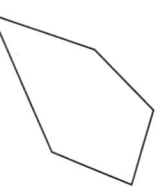 _____   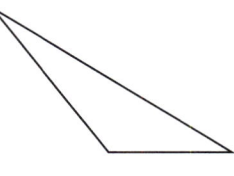 _____

3. 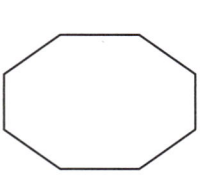 _____   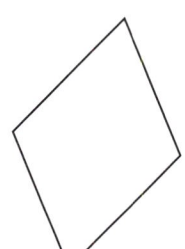 _____

Spectrum Geometry
Grade 5

Plane Figures

Identify each plane figure as a triangle, quadrilateral, pentagon, hexagon, heptagon, or octagon.

         a   b

1. 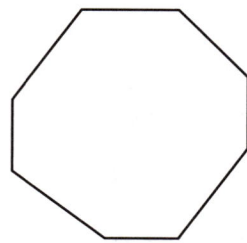   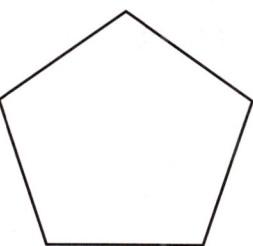

   _____   _____

2.    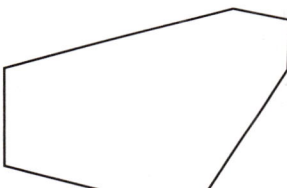

   _____   _____

3. 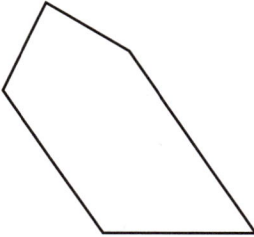   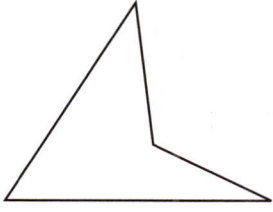

   _____   _____

NAME _____

SCORE ⬤ /3

Quadrilaterals

A **quadrilateral** is a polygon with four sides. Some examples are square, rectangle, parallelogram, rhombus, kite, and trapezoid.

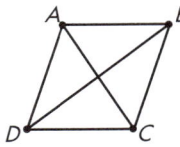 A **parallelogram** is a quadrilateral with opposite sides parallel and equal. ∠DAB = ∠BCD, ∠ADC = ∠CBA, $\overline{AB} = \overline{DC}$, $\overline{AD} = \overline{BC}$. $\overline{AC}$ bisects $\overline{BD}$. $\overline{BD}$ bisects $\overline{AC}$. △ADC is congruent to △CBA.

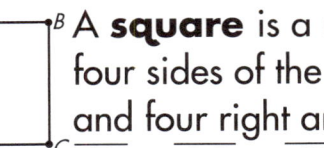 A **square** is a rectangle with four sides of the same length and four right angles. $\overline{AB} = \overline{BC} = \overline{CD} = \overline{DA}$. ∠ADC = ∠DCB = ∠CBA = ∠BAD.

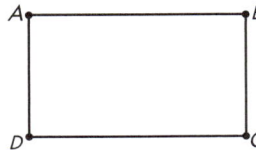 A **rectangle** is a parallelogram with four right angles. Opposite sides are equal. $\overline{AB} = \overline{DC}$, $\overline{AD} = \overline{BC}$, ∠BAD = ∠ABC = ∠BCD = ∠CDA = 90°.

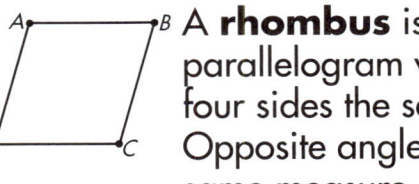 A **rhombus** is a parallelogram with all four sides the same length. Opposite angles are the same measure.

A **trapezoid** has just two sides that are parallel.

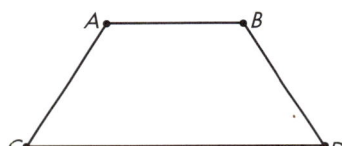

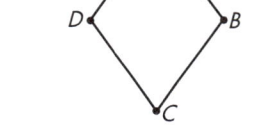 A **kite** has two pairs of adjacent sides that are congruent.

Identify each of the quadrilaterals.

a

1.

_____
Type

b

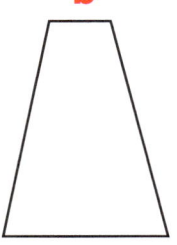

_____
Type

c

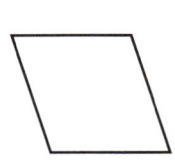

_____
Type

Spectrum Geometry
Grade 5

Chapter 3
Geometric Figures

26

NAME _____

SCORE ◯ / 6

Quadrilaterals

Use the figures below to answer each question. Letters may be used more than once. Some questions will have more than one answer. Some letters may not be used.

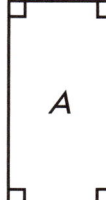 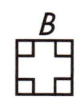  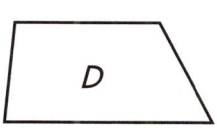 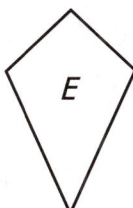 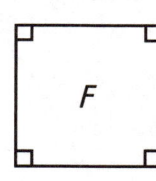

   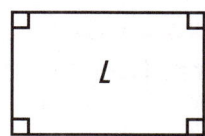 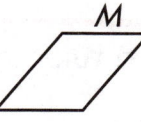

1. Which figure is a rectangle? _____

2. Which figure is a rhombus? _____

3. Which figure is a trapezoid? _____

4. Which figure is a square? _____

5. Which figure is a kite? _____

6. Which figure is a both a rhombus and a rectangle? _____

Spectrum Geometry
Grade 5

Chapter 3
Geometric Figures

27

Triangles

NAME _____

SCORE ⬜/6

An **equilateral** triangle has 3 sides of the same length.

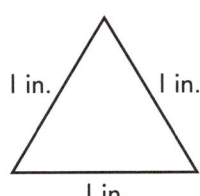

An **isosceles** triangle has at least 2 sides of the same length.

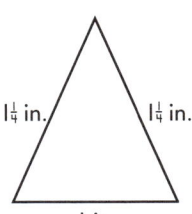

A **scalene** triangle has no sides of the same length.

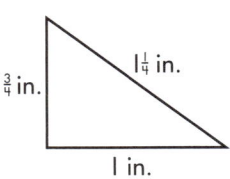

Use a ruler to measure. Label each triangle equilateral, isosceles, or scalene.

    a   **b**   **c**

1.

   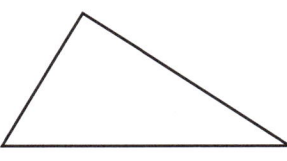   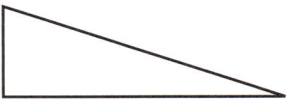

_____   _____   _____

2.

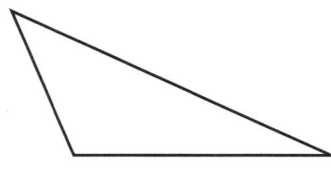   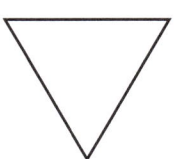

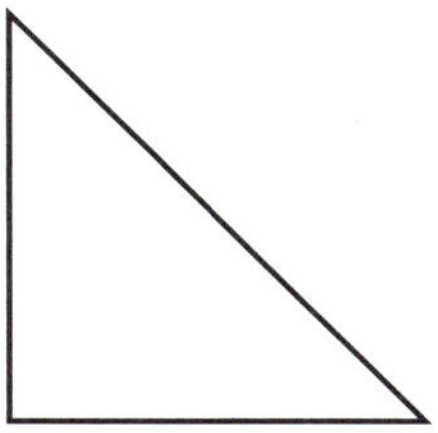

_____   _____   _____

Solid Figures

Solid figures are three-dimensional figures. They are named for the types of surfaces they have. These surfaces may be flat, curved, or both.

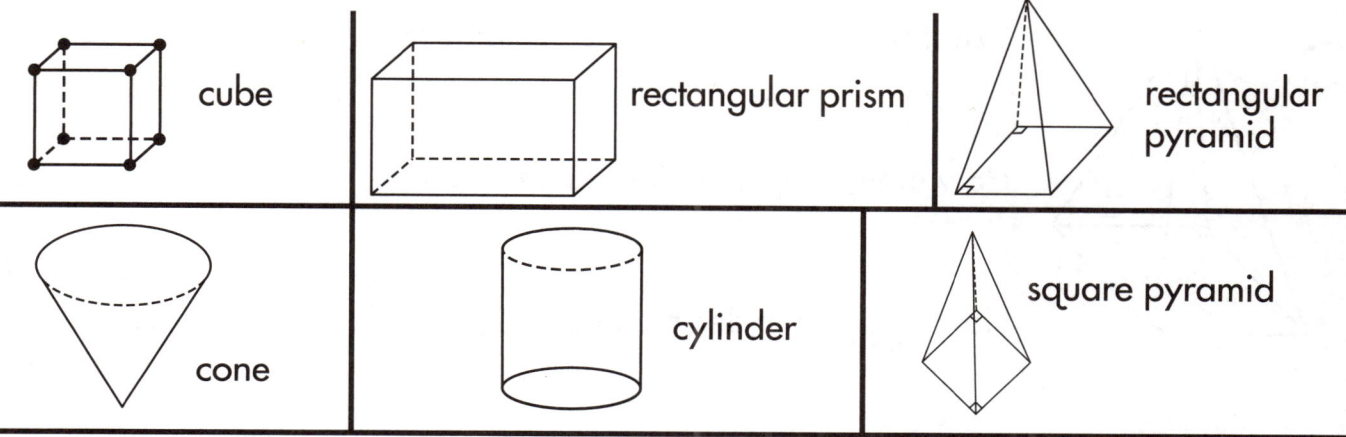

Solid figures have faces, edges, and vertices.

Answer the following questions.

1. What type of solid figure is this object? _____

    How many faces does it have? _____

    How many edges does it have? _____

    How many vertices does it have? _____

    What type of surfaces does it have? _____

Solid Figures

Answer the following questions.

1. 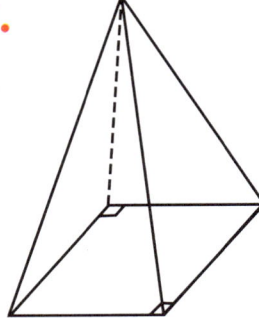 What type of solid figure is this object? _____

   How many edges does it have? _____

   How many triangles make up this figure? _____

   How many rectangles make up this figure? _____

   How many faces total? _____

   How many vertices? _____

2.  What type of solid figure is this object? _____

   How many circles does it have? _____

   What type of surfaces does it have? _____

Check What You Learned

Geometric Figures

Identify the following quadrilaterals.

      a   **b**

      Type   Type

1.  _____   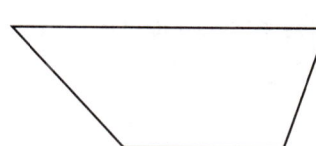 _____

2. 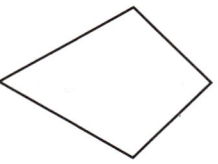 _____    _____

Match each figure with the number of the polygon.

3. triangle   _____

4. pentagon   _____       

5. heptagon   _____

Complete the information for each solid figure.

6. 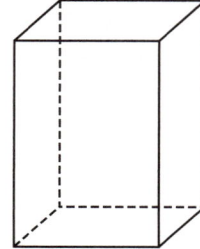   faces: _____   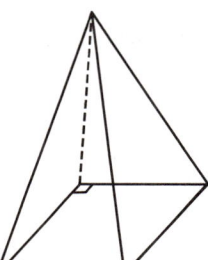   faces: _____

                            edges: _____   edges: _____

                            vertices: _____   vertices: _____

                            type: _____   type: _____

Spectrum Geometry
Grade 5

NAME _____

Check What You Know

Problem Solving: Geometric Figures

Read the problem carefully and solve. Show your work under each question.

Landscape designers draw artistic plans for gardens. The plans are drawn to scale so that people who install the landscapes can order what is needed. Designers often work with unusual shapes.

---

1. Designers create plans for a garden to fit a space like the one in the diagram. What is the name of this shape?

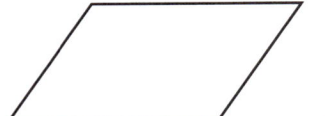 _____

2. Stepping stones in the Kwon garden are placed to look like the shape below. What is the name of this shape?

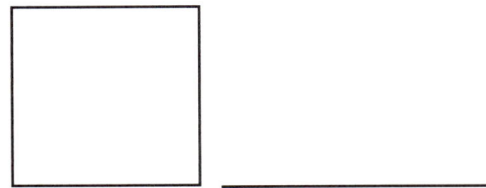 _____

3. The Patterson family wants a fountain that is shaped like the figure below. Describe the surfaces of the figure.

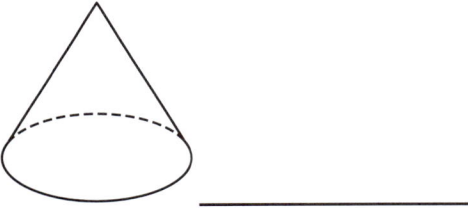 _____

4. Below is a plan for a section of patio at the Flores home. What is the name of this shape?

 _____

Spectrum Geometry
Grade 5

NAME _____

SCORE ___ / 5

Solid Figures

Read the problem carefully and solve. Show your work under each question.

Two of Mr. Solomon's fifth-grade math classes build models of solid figures. Students will get rewards for skillful work and good ideas. The students can make the models out of any materials they want to use.

Use this diagram to answer questions 1 and 2.

1. David uses clay to make a model of this solid. What is the name of this figure?

   _____

2. Hannah notices something interesting about this object. What shape are the faces on the two ends of the solid?

   _____

Use this diagram to answer question 3.

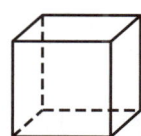

3. Another student looks carefully at the solid. How many edges does this solid have? How many faces and vertices does it have?

   It has _____ edges, _____ faces, and _____ vertices.

Spectrum Geometry
Grade 5

Chapter 4
Problem Solving: Geometric Figures

33

Quadrilaterals

Read the problem carefully and solve. Show your work under each question.

Students in the Freestone School look at a map. The map is made from high altitude photographs of farms near Freestone. The map shows some odd shapes. The shapes are all four-sided figures called *quadrilaterals*.

Helpful Hint

A **parallelogram** has parallel opposite sides.

A **rectangle** is a parallelogram with four right angles.

A **square** is a rectangle with four equal sides.

A **rhombus** is a parallelogram that has four equal sides.

A **trapezoid** has just two parallel sides.

A **kite** has two pairs of sides next to each other that are the same length.

1. Jessica points to a farm on the map that is shaped like the figure in the diagram. What is this figure called?

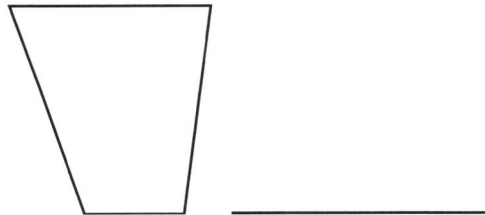

2. Daniel sees a farm that has the shape shown below. What is this shape called?

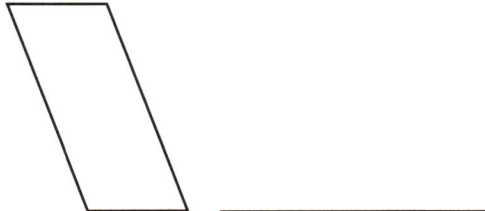

NAME _____

Quadrilaterals

SCORE ⬜/2

3. The shape of a field is shown in the diagram. What is the name of this shape?

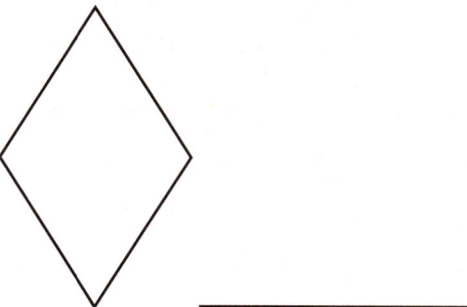 _____

4. The diagram below shows the shape of a field that Cameron finds on a map. What is the name of this shape?

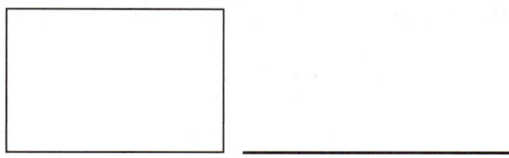 _____

Polygons

Read the problem carefully and solve. Show your work under each question.

Ms. Leon's children are bored on a rainy day. She tells her children to cut out geometric shapes to make designs on poster board. The shapes are all polygons.

Helpful Hint

A **triangle** has 3 sides.

A **quadrilateral** has 4 sides.

A **pentagon** has 5 sides.

A **hexagon** has 6 sides.

A **heptagon** has 7 sides.

An **octagon** has 8 sides.

1. Aimee cuts some construction paper into shapes like the one below. What is the name of this polygon?

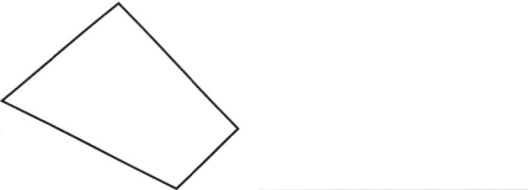

2. Rudy uses pieces of thin cardboard to make designs. One piece looks like the shape below. What is the name of this polygon?

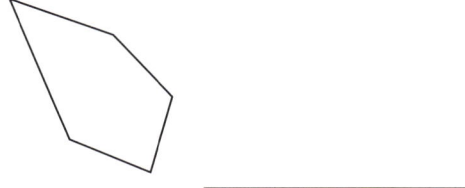

Polygons

SCORE /3

3. Renee cuts some cardboard to create shapes. One of the shapes looks like the diagram below. What is the name of this shape?

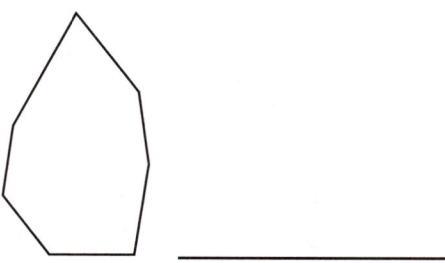
_____

4. Connie makes shapes using colored paper. One cutout looks like the shape below. What is the name of this shape?

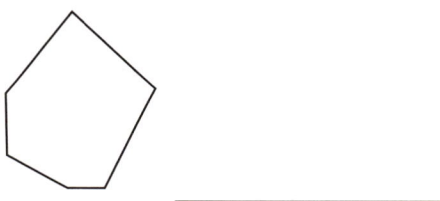
_____

5. Ms. Leon cuts out a big piece of poster board in the shape shown below. What is the name of this shape?

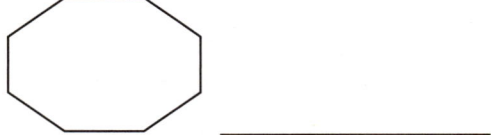
_____

NAME _____

Check What You Learned

Problem Solving: Geometric Figures

Read the problem carefully and solve. Show your work under each question.

Interior decorators use many different objects to make homes look more beautiful. Some of these objects have the shapes of flat geometric figures. Others have the shapes of solids.

1. Ms. Holmes decorates a child's bedroom with a set of colorful panels like the one shown below. What is the shape of these panels?

   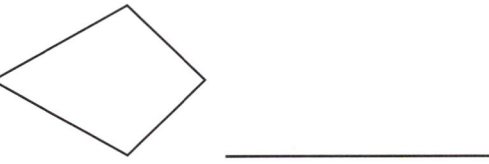
   _____

2. Mr. Porter found a clock for a customer. The clock looks like the solid below. What is the name of this solid? How many vertices does it have?

   _____
   _____ vertices

3. Mr. Larson uses a large cabinet. The shape of the cabinet is shown below. What is the name of this shape? How many faces does it have? How many edges does it have?

   _____
   _____ faces
   _____ edges

Spectrum Geometry
Grade 5

Mid-Test Chapters 1–4

Write the name of each angle. Use a protractor to measure each angle.

a **b**

1.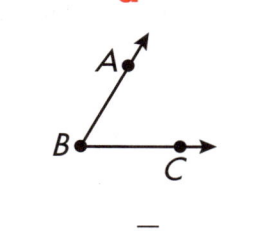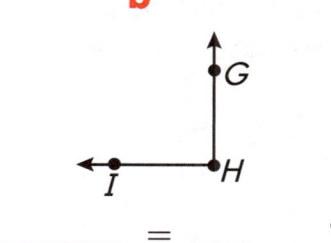

∠ _____ = _____°   ∠ _____ = _____°

Draw and name the following figures.

2. line OP   • O   • P   _____

3. ray RS   • R   • S   _____

Find the measure of each angle of the given triangle. Label each angle as right, acute, or obtuse.

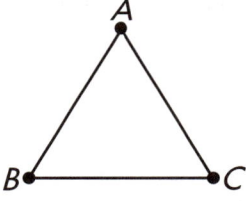 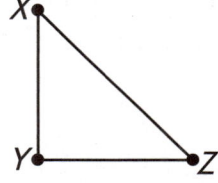

4. ∠ _____ = _____°   ∠ _____ = _____°

It is _____.   It is _____.

∠ _____ = _____°   ∠ _____ = _____°

It is _____.   It is _____.

∠ _____ = _____°   ∠ _____ = _____°

It is _____.   It is _____.

Spectrum Geometry
Grade 5

Mid-Test: Chapters 1–4

Read each problem carefully and solve.

5. Zoey makes a collage using pieces of paper shaped like the figure below. What is the shape of the paper?

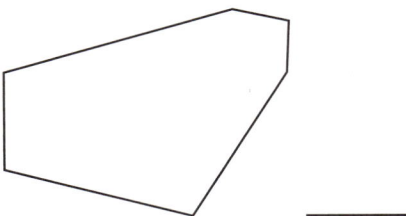

_____

6. Chris wants to build a model shaped like the figure below. What is the name of this solid?

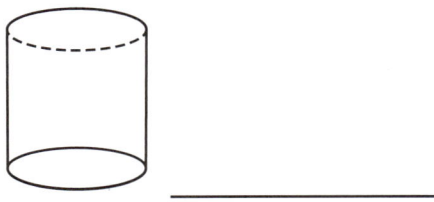

_____

7. The shape of a tile that is used for decoration in the Tai home is shown below. What is the name of the shape?

_____

8. Ming is drawing a pathway through her grandma's garden. She draws two lines that intersect and form a right angle at a single point. The lines are AB and KJ. They cross at point D. Draw and label a diagram of the two lines. What kind of lines are these?

_____

NAME _____

Check What You Know

Perimeter, Area, and Volume

Find the perimeter of each figure.

1.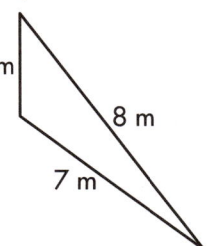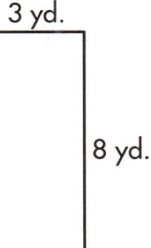

perimeter = _____ m   perimeter = _____ yd.   perimeter = _____ ft.

Find the area of each rectangle.

2.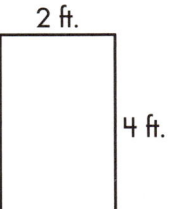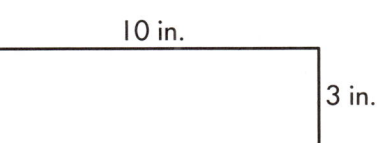

area = _____ sq. ft.   area = _____ sq. in.   area = _____ sq. cm

Find the volume of each rectangular solid.

3.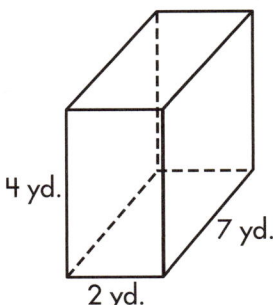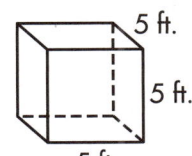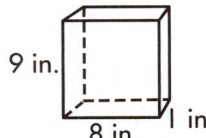

_____ cubic yd.   _____ cubic ft.   _____ cubic in.

Spectrum Geometry
Grade 5

Chapter 5
Perimeter, Area, and Volume

41

CHAPTER 5 PRETEST

NAME _____

Measuring Perimeter

The **perimeter** is the sum of the sides of a figure.

To find the perimeter, add the length of the sides.

```
  6         6 × 2 = 12      1 2
  5     or  5 × 2 = 10    + 1 0
  6                         2 2
+ 5
 2 2
```

The perimeter of the rectangle is ___22___ in.

Find the perimeter of each figure.

           a   **b**

1. 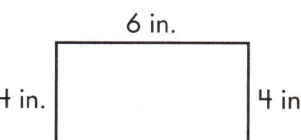 _____ in. 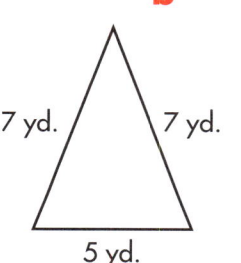 _____ yd.

2. 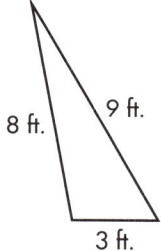 _____ ft. 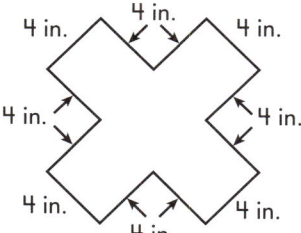 _____ in.

3. 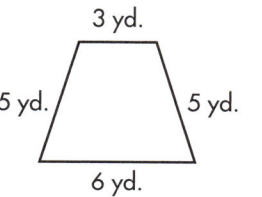 _____ yd. 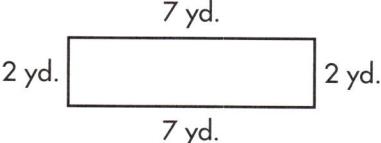 _____ yd.

Spectrum Geometry
Grade 5

Measuring Perimeter

SCORE /6

Find the perimeter of each figure.

           a   **b**

1. 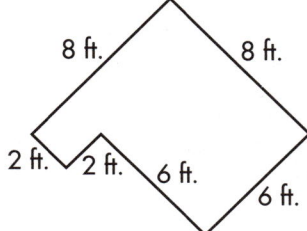   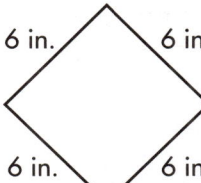

_____ ft.   _____ in.

2.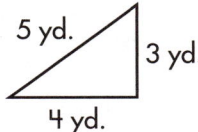

_____ yd.   _____ ft.

3. 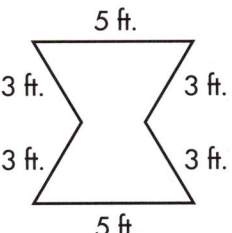   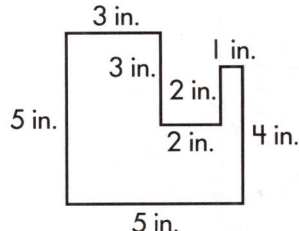

_____ ft.   _____ in.

Spectrum Geometry
Grade 5

NAME _____

Measuring Perimeter

Find the perimeter of each figure.

      a   **b**

1.

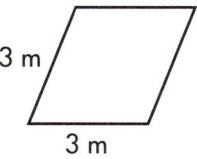

       _____ m   _____ in.

2.

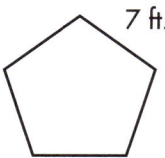

       _____ ft.   _____ yd.

3.

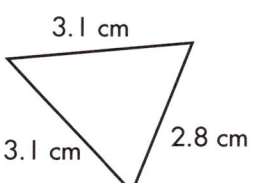

       _____ cm   _____ m

Spectrum Geometry
Grade 5

NAME _____

SCORE ⬭ /6

Measuring Area

Area is the number of square units needed to cover a surface.

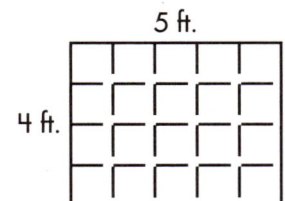

To calculate the area of a square or rectangle, multiply the measure of the length by the measure of the width.

Length: 5 ft.   5 ft.
Width: 4 ft.   × 4 ft.
                 20 square feet

The area of a rectangle 5 feet in length and 4 feet in width is __20 square feet__.

Find the area of each rectangle.

        a   **b**

1. 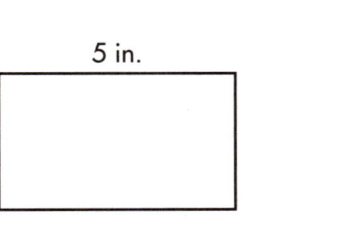 _____ sq. in.   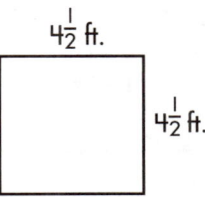 _____ sq. ft.

2. 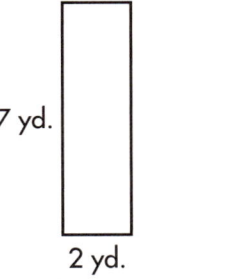 _____ sq. yd.   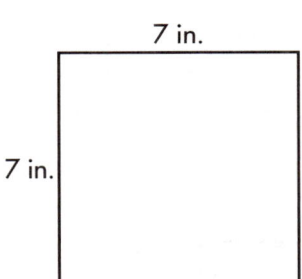 _____ sq. in.

3.  _____ sq. ft.    _____ sq. in.

Spectrum Geometry
Grade 5

NAME _____

Measuring Area

Find the area or missing length for each rectangle.

        a   **b**

1.

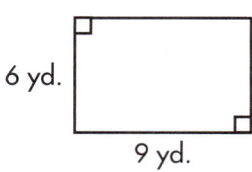

                                                                         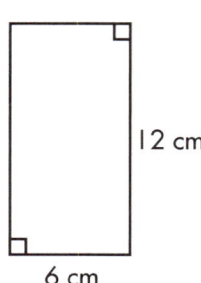

area = _____ yd.²   area = _____ cm²

2.

10 km   A = 150 km²

                                                                         A = 100 m²

length = _____ km   length = _____ m

3.

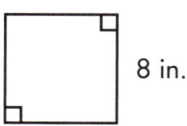   8 in.   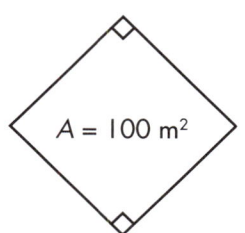 A = 256 ft.²   8 ft.

area = _____ in.²   length = _____ ft.

Spectrum Geometry
Grade 5

NAME _____

SCORE ⬚ / 8

Measuring Perimeter and Area

Find the perimeter or area of each figure.

         a   **b**

1.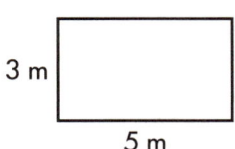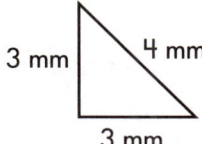

area = _____ m²   perimeter = _____ mm

2.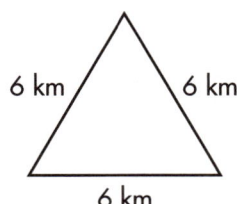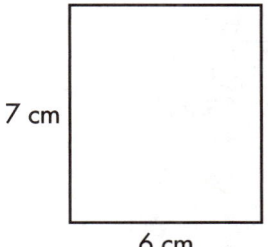

perimeter = _____ km   area = _____ cm²

3.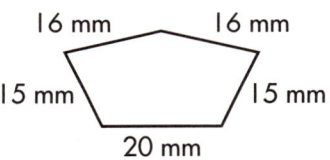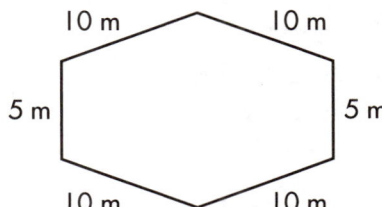

perimeter = _____ mm   perimeter = _____ m

4.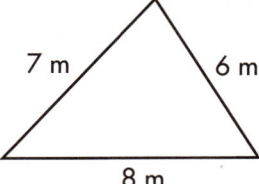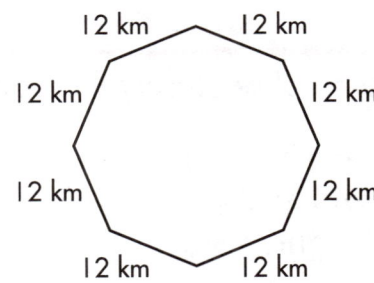

perimeter = _____ m   perimeter = _____ km

Spectrum Geometry
Grade 5

NAME _____

Measuring Volume

Volume is the number of cubic units needed to fill a given solid.

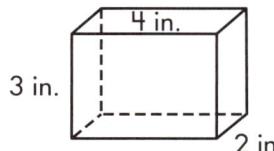

Length: 4 in.   Volume = length × width × height
Width: 2 in.   Volume = (4 in.) × (2 in.) × (3 in.)
Height: 3 in.
                Volume = ____24____ cubic inches

Find the volume of each rectangular solid.

        a   **b**   **c**

1. 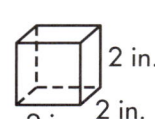   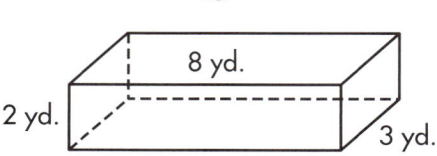   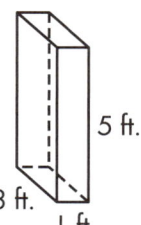

_____ cu. in.   _____ cu. yd.   _____ cu. ft.

2. 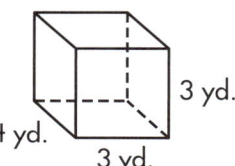   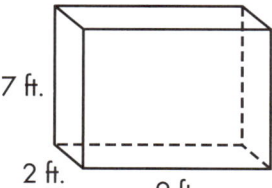   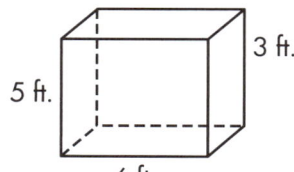

_____ cu. yd.   _____ cu. ft.   _____ cu. ft.

Find the volume of each rectangular solid with the given measurements.

3.   length: 7 yd.   length: 3 ft.   length: 5 in.
       width: 2 yd.   width: 6 ft.   width: 4 in.
       height: 4 yd.   height: 8 ft.   height: 7 in.

_____ cu. yd.   _____ cu. ft.   _____ cu. ft.

NAME _____

SCORE ___/6

Measuring Volume

The **volume of a rectangular solid** is the product of the length times width times height. The product of the length times width is the base. The formula for the volume is V = B × h. Because volume is measured in 3 dimensions, it is expressed in **cubic units** or **units3**.

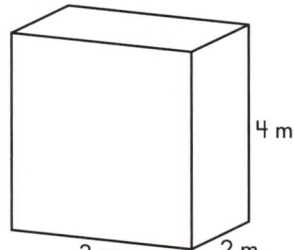

B = 3 × 2 = 6
V = B × h = 6 × 4
V = 24 m³

Find the volume of each rectangular solid.

        a   **b**   **c**

1.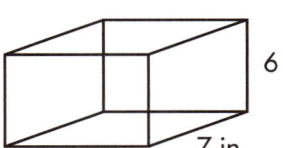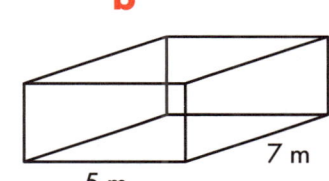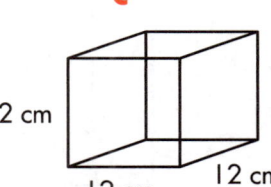

   _____ in.³   _____ m³   _____ cm³

2.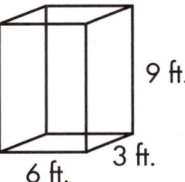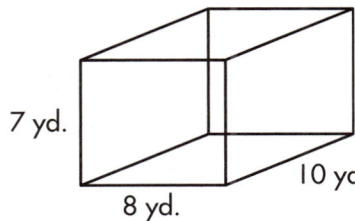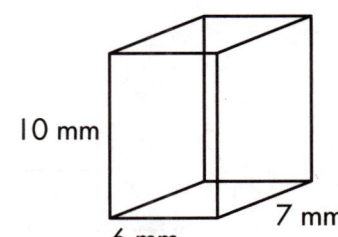

   _____ ft.³   _____ yd.³   _____ mm³

Spectrum Geometry
Grade 5

Chapter 5
Perimeter, Area, and Volume

NAME _____

Measuring Volume

Find the volume of each figure.

        a   **b**

1. 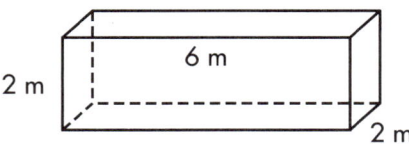   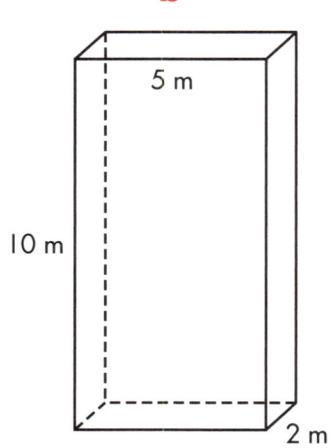

_____ cubic meters   _____ cubic meters

2. 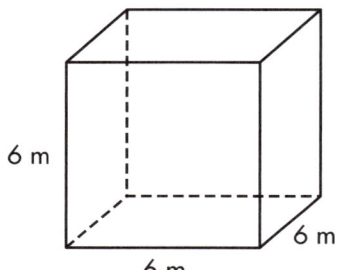   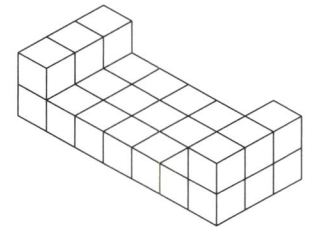

_____ cubic meters   _____ cubic units

3. 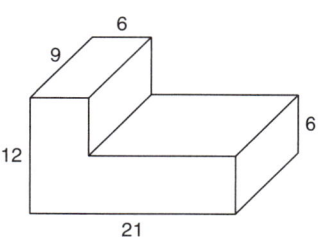   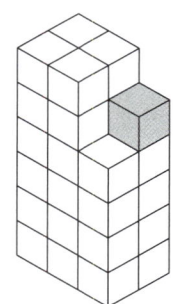

_____ cubic units   _____ cubic units

Measuring Volume

SCORE /6

Find the volume of each figure.

          a   **b**

1.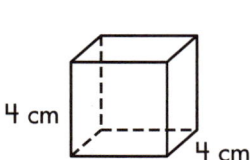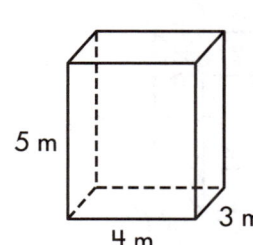

_____ cubic centimeters   _____ cubic meters

2.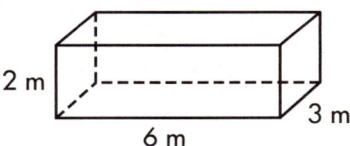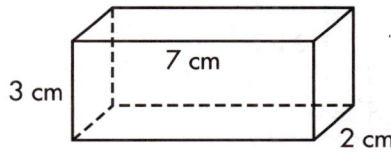

_____ cubic meters   _____ cubic centimeters

3.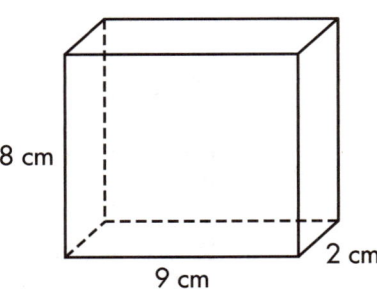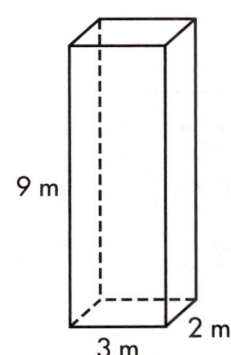

_____ cubic centimeters   _____ cubic meters

Spectrum Geometry
Grade 5

NAME _____

SCORE ⬜/9

Measuring Volume

Find the volume of each figure.

a   b   c

1.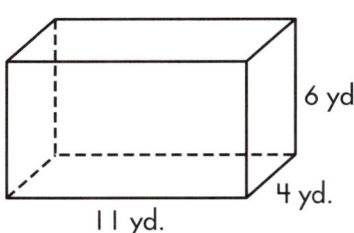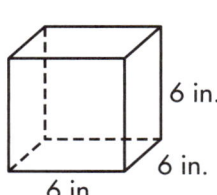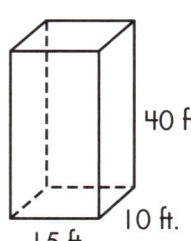

_____ cubic yards   _____ cubic inches   _____ cubic feet

2.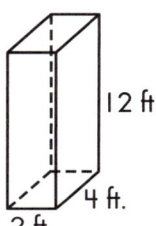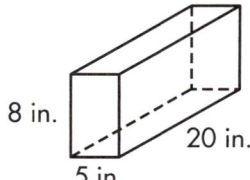

_____ cubic feet   _____ cubic inches   _____ cubic inches

3.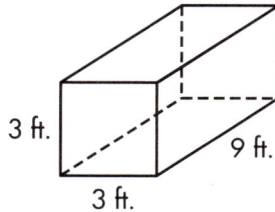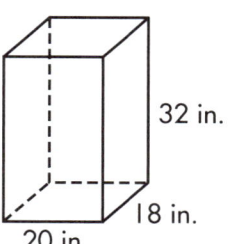

_____ cubic feet   _____ cubic inches   _____ cubic inches

Spectrum Geometry
Grade 5

Check What You Learned

Perimeter, Area, and Volume

NAME _____

Find the area of each figure.

a **b** **c**

1.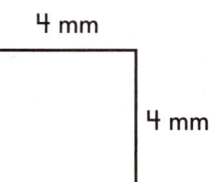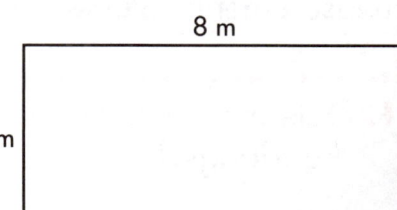

area = _____ sq. mm   area = _____ sq. m   area = _____ sq. m

2.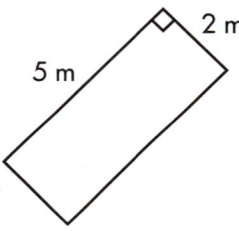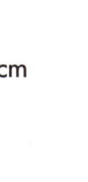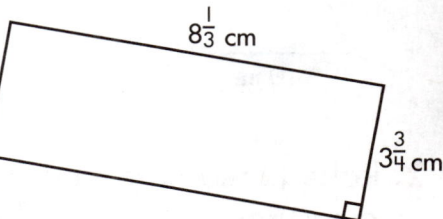

area = _____ sq. m   area = _____ sq. cm   area = _____ sq. cm

Find the volume of each rectangular solid with the given measurements.

3. length: 4 m   length: 7 m   length: 8 m
    width: 2 m   width: 2 m   width: 8 m
    height: 8 m   height: 6 m   height: 8 m

volume = ____ cubic m   volume = ____ cubic m   volume = ____ cubic m

Find the perimeter of each figure.

4.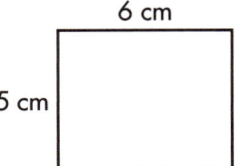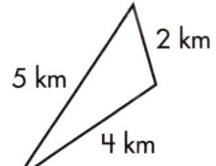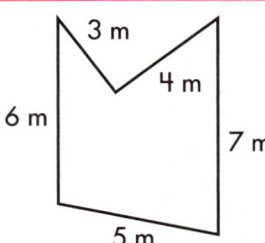

perimeter = _____ cm   perimeter = _____ km   perimeter = _____ m

Spectrum Geometry
Grade 5

Chapter 5
Perimeter, Area, and Volume

53

NAME _____

Check What You Know

Problem Solving: Perimeter, Area, and Volume

Read the problem carefully and solve. Show your work under each question.

In the Tyler Middle School science classes, the students learn how to take measurements. Students measure the size of fixed objects in the classroom.

---

1. Dale measures the perimeter of the triangle below. What is the perimeter of the triangle?

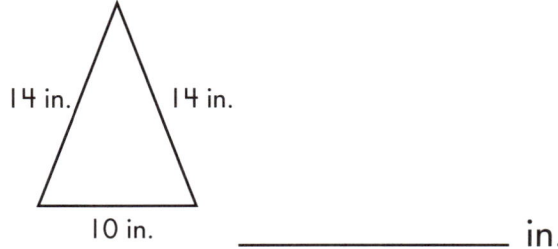

_____ in.

2. Robert measures the length and the width of the classroom. The rectangular room measures 9 yards by 7 yards. What is the area of the room?

_____ sq. yd.

3. Yolanda measures the volume of a pencil box below. What is its volume?

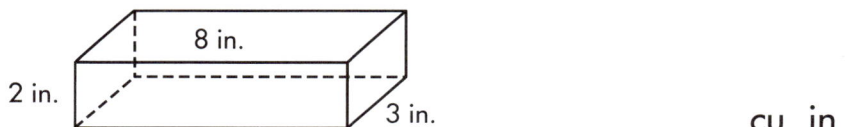

_____ cu. in.

4. Sasha stacks some cubes into the figure below. What is the volume?

_____ cubic units

Spectrum Geometry
Grade 5
54

NAME _____

SCORE ◯ /2

Measuring Perimeter and Area

Read the problem carefully and solve. Show your work under each question.

The Highland Paving Company paves areas ranging from a few square feet to many square yards. The company has special rates for paving small areas. The manager makes a scale drawing for each job so he knows how much material is needed to complete the project.

> **Helpful Hint**
>
> **Perimeter** is the sum of the sides of a figure.
>
> **Area** is the number of square units that cover a surface. To find the area of a rectangle or square, multiply the length times the width.

1. A place to park bicycles at a school is in the shape of a triangle. What is the perimeter of the triangle?

   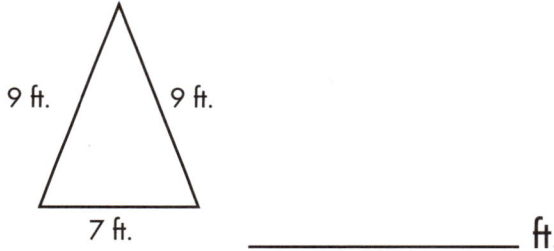

   9 ft.   9 ft.

   7 ft.   _____ ft.

2. The diagram below shows the area of an old sidewalk that needs to be repaved. What is the area of the sidewalk?

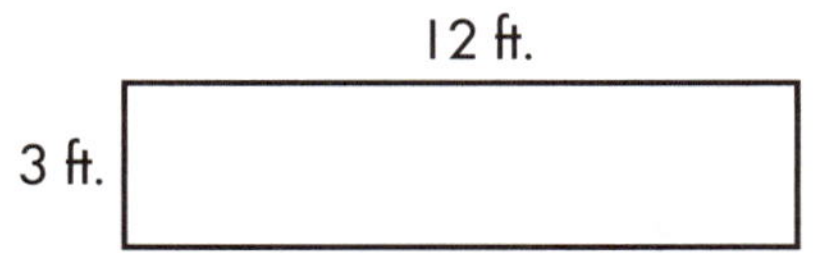

   12 ft.

   3 ft.   _____ sq. ft.

Spectrum Geometry
Grade 5

Chapter 6
Problem Solving: Perimeter, Area, and Volume

55

NAME _____

SCORE ⬚ / 2

Measuring Perimeter and Area

Read the problem carefully and solve. Show your work under each question.

The Highland Paving Company paves areas ranging from a few square feet to many square yards. The company has special rates for paving small areas. The manager makes a scale drawing for each job so he knows how much material is needed to complete the project.

---

1. The diagram below is a scale drawing of a paving project. To finish the paving, it needs edging. What is the perimeter of the project?

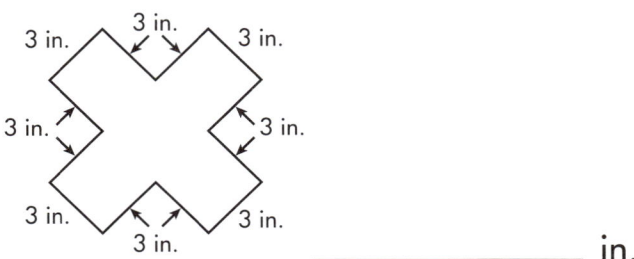

_____ in.

2. The diagram shows a driveway that will be paved. What is the area of the driveway?

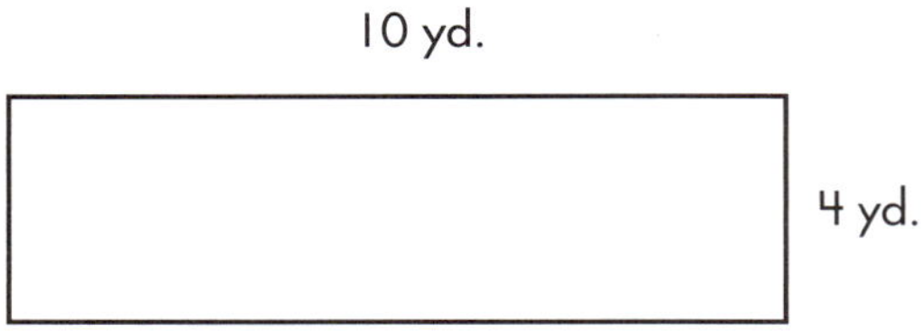

10 yd.

4 yd.

_____ sq. yd.

Spectrum Geometry
Grade 5

NAME _____

SCORE ☐ /3

Measuring Perimeter and Area

Read the problem carefully and solve. Show your work under each question.

In Ms. Simon's art class, students decorate shoe boxes. The project encourages students to be creative and think of new ideas. Each shoe box measures 18 cm wide, 12 cm tall, and 28 cm long.

---

1. Kathy cuts a piece of colored paper to go on the top of the shoe box. What is the area of the paper she cuts?

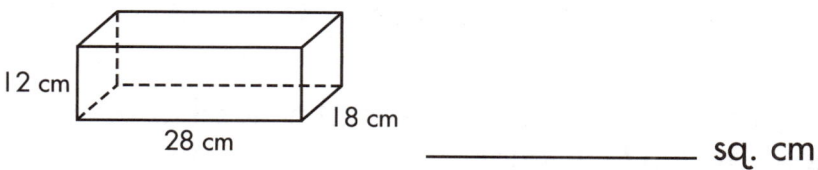

_____ sq. cm

2. Linnell wants to put a ribbon around the top of the box. What is the perimeter of the top?

_____ cm

3. Tom cuts small triangles to use as box decorations. What is the perimeter of each triangle in millimeters?

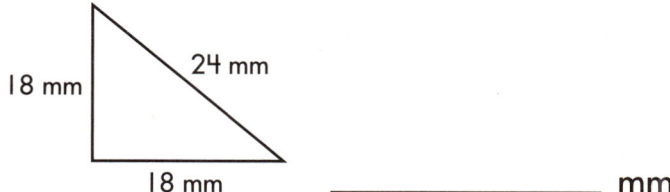

_____ mm

Spectrum Geometry
Grade 5

Chapter 6
Problem Solving: Perimeter, Area, and Volume

57

NAME _____

SCORE ◯ /2

Measuring Perimeter and Area

Read the problem carefully and solve. Show your work under each question.

In Ms. Simon's art class, students decorate shoe boxes. The project encourages students to be creative and think of new ideas. Each shoe box measures 18 cm wide, 12 cm tall, and 28 cm long.

> **Helpful Hint**
>
> The **perimeter** is the distance around an object. The perimeter is the sum of the lengths of the sides.
>
> The **area** of an object is the number of **square units** (sq.) needed to cover it. To find the area of a rectangle, multiply the length of the rectangle times the width.

1. Ms. Simon has a roll of wrapping paper. A piece 60 centimeters long is used to wrap one box. How many meters of wrapping paper are needed to wrap 100 boxes?

   _____ m

2. Patrick makes rectangles for decorations. The rectangles measure 2 centimeters by 3 centimeters. What is the total area of 50 rectangles?

   _____ sq. cm

Spectrum Geometry
Grade 5

Measuring Volume

SCORE / 2

Read the problem carefully and solve. Show your work under each question.

The Pack-It Box Company makes boxes and crates. The boxes range from a few inches on a side to several feet. The crates range from a few feet to a few yards.

Helpful Hint

Volume is the number of cubic (cu.) units that fill a solid object. To find the volume of a solid with rectangular sides, multiply the length, width, and height together.

1. Boris puts together a big crate for a large piece of office furniture. What is the volume of this crate?

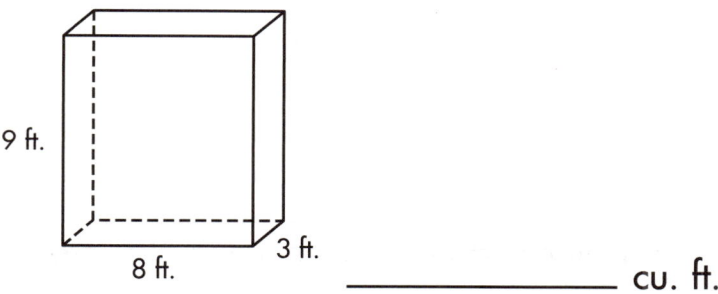

_____ cu. ft.

2. Victor designs a box for a company that makes mirrors. What is the volume of the box he designs?

_____ cu. ft.

Spectrum Geometry
Grade 5

Chapter 6
Problem Solving: Perimeter, Area, and Volume

NAME _____

SCORE ⬚ / 3

Measuring Volume

Read the problem carefully and solve. Show your work under each question.

The Pack-It Box Company makes boxes and crates. The boxes range from a few inches on a side to several feet. The crates range from a few feet to a few yards.

1. Pack-It's watch box is a cube. What is the volume of the box?

   _____ cu. in.

2. Pam prepares boxes for a toy company. What is the volume of each box?

   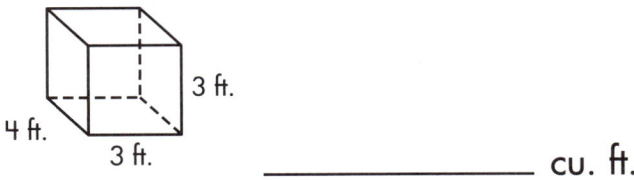

   _____ cu. ft.

3. Karen builds a crate to ship a huge machine. What is the volume of the crate?

   _____ cu. yd.

Spectrum Geometry
Grade 5

Chapter 6
Problem Solving: Perimeter, Area, and Volume

NAME _____

SCORE / 2

Measuring Volume

Read the problem carefully and solve. Show your work under each question.

Quiet Air Company supplies heating and air-conditioning services. The company measures the volume of each room to supply the correct amount of heat and cool air throughout a building.

Helpful Hint

To find the **volume** of a space with sides shaped like rectangles, multiply the measure of the length, the width, and the height or multiply the measure of the base (length × width) and height.

Cubic units (cu.) are used for volumes.

1. The diagram below shows the measurements of a room the company will heat. What is the volume of the room?

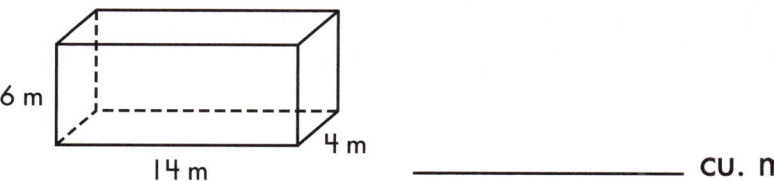

_____ cu. m

2. The diagram below shows the dimensions of a space for an air conditioner. What is the volume of this space?

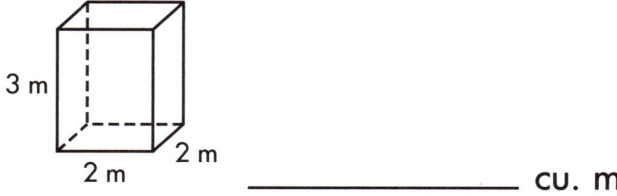

_____ cu. m

Spectrum Geometry
Grade 5

Chapter 6
Problem Solving: Perimeter, Area, and Volume

NAME _____

SCORE ◯/2

Measuring Volume

Read the problem carefully and solve. Show your work under each question.

Quiet Air Company supplies heating and air-conditioning services. The company measures the volume of each room to supply the correct amount of heat and cool air throughout a building.

1. The diagram below shows the measurements of the entrance to an office building. What is the volume of the entrance?

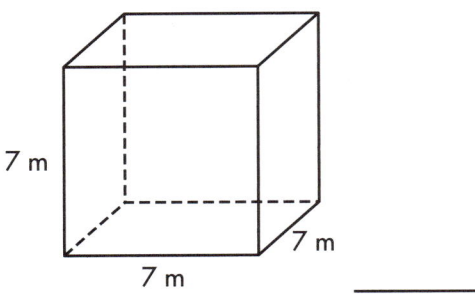

_____ cu. m

2. A wall thermostat controls the temperature in a room. The thermostat has the dimensions shown in the diagram below. What is the volume of the thermostat?

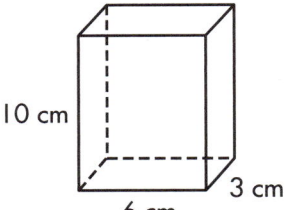

_____ cu. cm

Spectrum Geometry
Grade 5

Chapter 6
Problem Solving: Perimeter, Area, and Volume

Check What You Learned

Problem Solving: Perimeter, Area, and Volume

Read the problem carefully and solve. Show your work under each question.

The Pleasant Living Home Store sells many products that make homes more enjoyable. Some products are ready to use. Other products, like paint, have to be applied or installed in the home.

---

1. Rochelle measures the volume of a room to decide how much air freshener to use. What is its volume?

   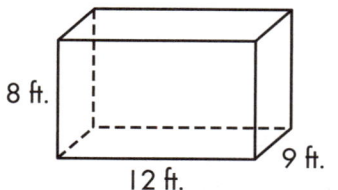

   _____ cu. ft.

2. Charlie wants to repaint one wall in a room. The wall measures 9 feet tall by 14 feet long. What is the area of the wall?

   _____ sq. ft.

3. Helen measures the size of a room to see if a certain rug will fit in the room. What is the perimeter and area of the room?

   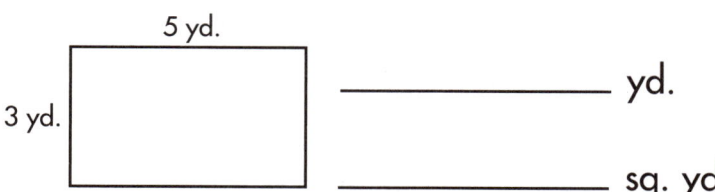

   _____ yd.

   _____ sq. yd.

4. Carter wants the store to design a figure like the one shown below to display on his bookcase. What is the volume?

   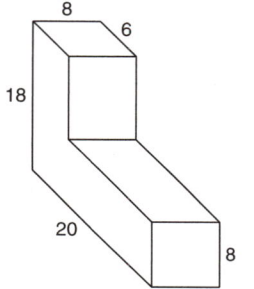

   _____ cubic units

Spectrum Geometry
Grade 5

Check What You Know

The Coordinate Plane

Use the grid to name a point for each ordered pair.

       a   **b**

1. (2, 6) _____   (6, 5) _____

2. (2, 2) _____   (4, 7) _____

Using the same grid, name the ordered pair for each point.

3. E (____, ____)   B (____, ____)

4. D (____, ____)   G (____, ____)

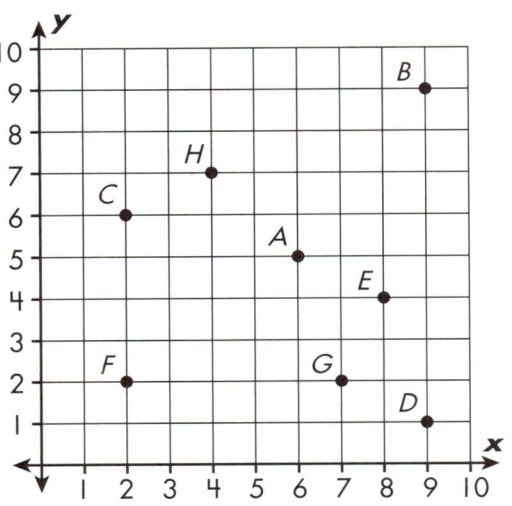

Plot the points shown on the grid. Label the points.

       a   **b**

5. M (4, 4)   N (3, 6)

6. O (6, 7)   P (5, 4)

7. Q (3, 1)   R (9, 2)

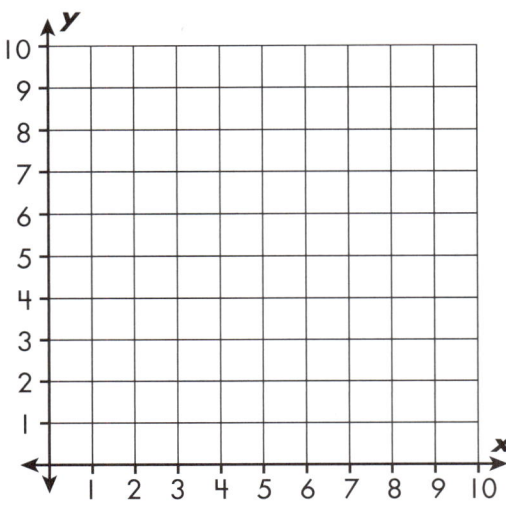

Spectrum Geometry
Grade 5

Ordered Pairs on a Coordinate Plane

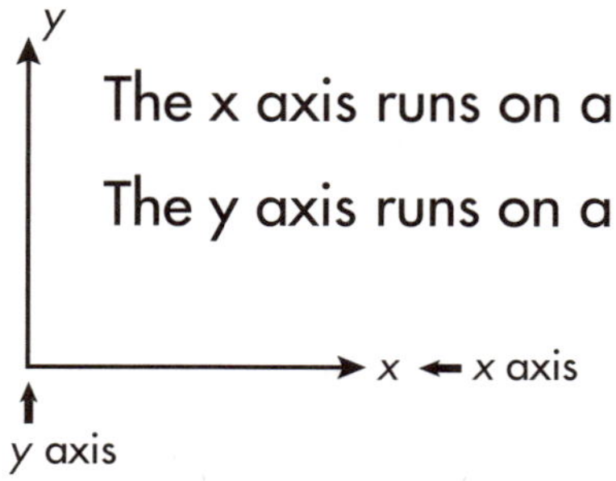

The x axis runs on a horizontal line.

The y axis runs on a vertical line.

Points located on the same grid are called **coordinate points**, or **coordinates**.

A point on a grid is located by using an ordered pair. An ordered pair lists an x axis point first and then a y axis point.

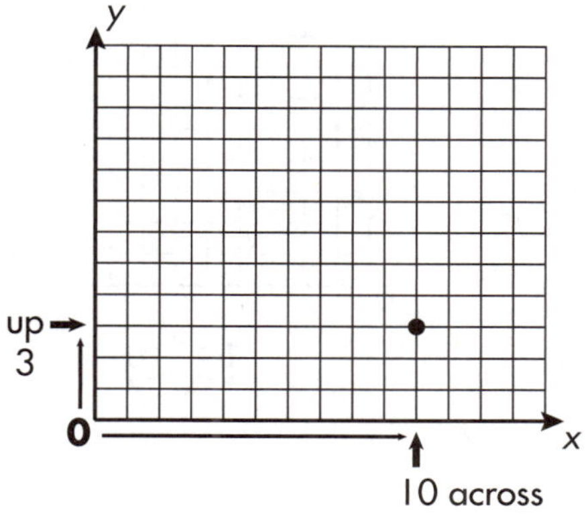

(10, 3)

   x y

First: Count across ten lines.

Second: From that point, go up three.

Third: Draw a point.

Identify the ordered pair from each grid.

a   **b**

1.
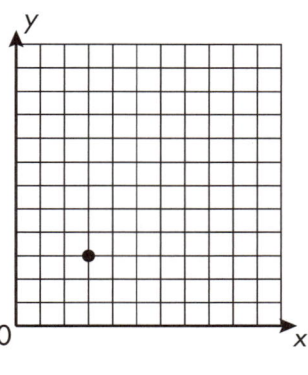 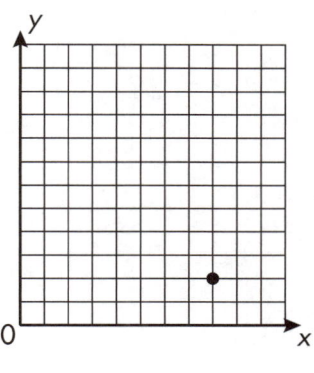

_____ _____

Spectrum Geometry
Grade 5

Chapter 7
The Coordinate Plane

NAME _____

Ordered Pairs on a Coordinate Plane

Plot each ordered pair.

1.

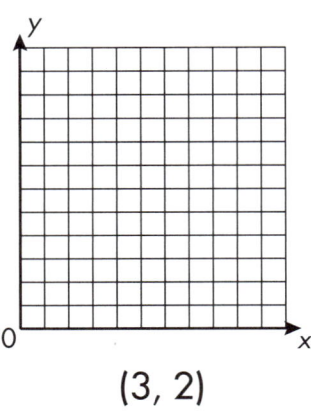

(3, 2)

2.

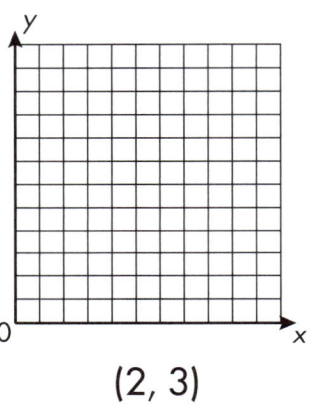

(2, 3)

3.

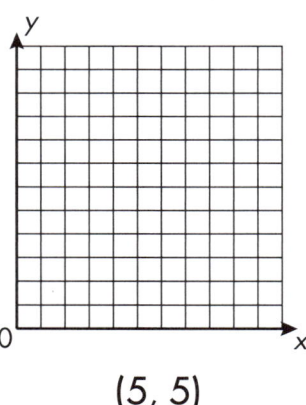

(5, 5)

Spectrum Geometry
Grade 5

Chapter 7
The Coordinate Plane

Plotting Ordered Pairs

The position of any point on a grid can be described by an **ordered pair** of numbers. The two numbers are named in order: (x, y). Point A on the grid at the right is named by the ordered pair (3, 2). It is located at 3 on the horizontal scale (x) and at 2 on the vertical scale (y). The number on the horizontal scale is always named first in an ordered pair. Point B is named by the ordered pair (7, 3).

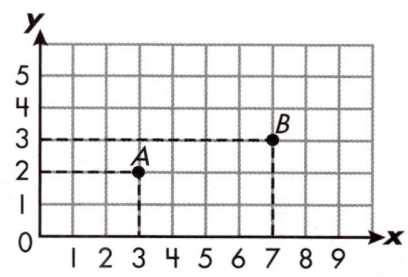

Use the grid to name the point for each ordered pair.

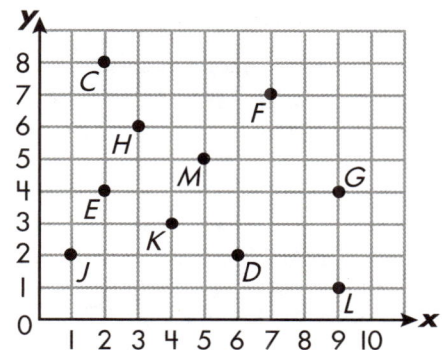

1. (1, 2) _____   (2, 4) _____

2. (3, 6) _____   (9, 4) _____

3. (9, 1) _____   (5, 5) _____

4. (2, 8) _____   (4, 3) _____

5. (7, 7) _____   (6, 2) _____

Plotting Ordered Pairs

Use the grid to name the point for each ordered pair.

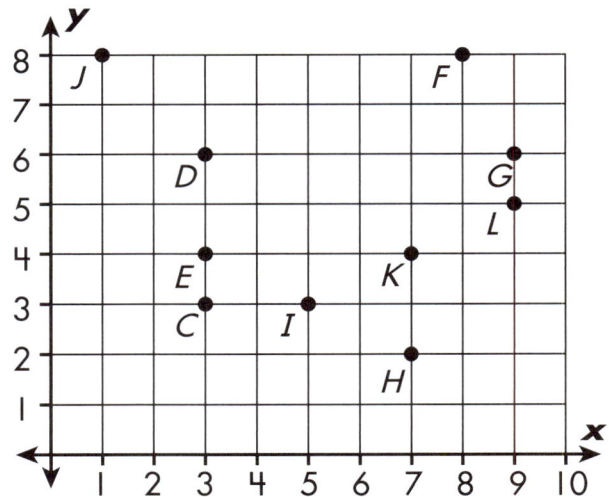

1. (7, 2) _____   (3, 4) _____

2. (3, 6) _____   (9, 6) _____

3. L (____, ____)   C (____, ____)

4. J (____, ____)   I (____, ____)

5. F (____, ____)   K (____, ____)

Spectrum Geometry
Grade 5

Plotting Ordered Pairs

Plot each ordered pair on the grid.

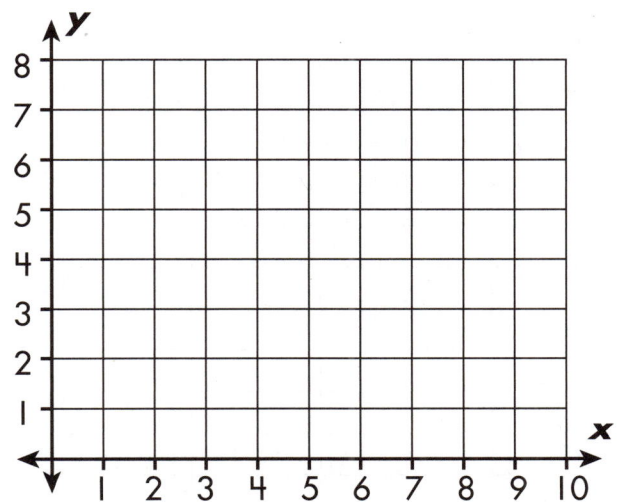

1.   A(1, 5)   B(5, 3)

2.   C(7, 4)   D(2, 2)

3.   E(4, 7)   F(9, 1)

4.   G(8, 2)   H(7, 6)

5.   I(6, 5)   J(1, 7)

Spectrum Geometry
Grade 5

Chapter 7
The Coordinate Plane

Plotting Ordered Pairs

Plot each ordered pair on the grid.

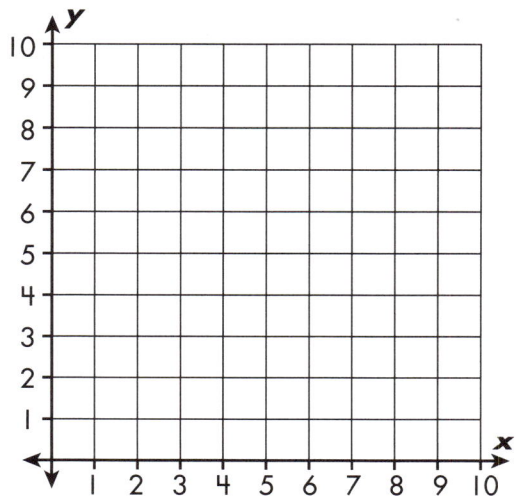

1.   A(4, 5)   B(8, 4)

2.   C(2, 3)   D(2, 2)

3.   E(7, 1)   F(7, 8)

4.   G(6, 4)   H(8, 3)

5.   I(1, 1)   J(4, 7)

Spectrum Geometry
Grade 5

NAME _____

SCORE ⬯/20

Plotting Ordered Pairs

Write where each lettered point is located on the grid.

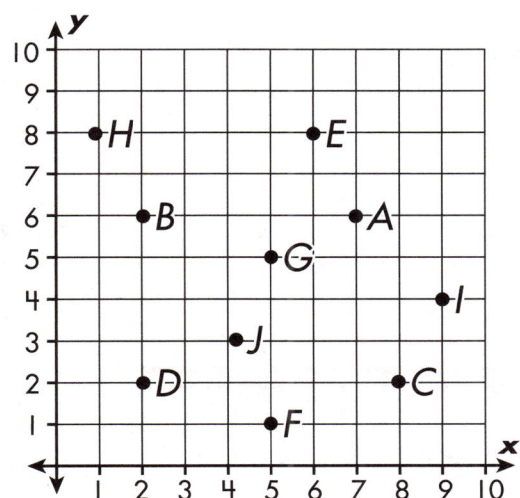

1. A (___ , ___)   B (___ , ___)

2. C (___ , ___)   D (___ , ___)

3. E (___ , ___)   F (___ , ___)

4. G (___ , ___)   H (___ , ___)

5. I (___ , ___)   J (___ , ___)

NAME _____

SCORE ⬤ /2

Plotting Ordered Pairs

Read the problem carefully and solve. Show your work under each question.

Lee graphed and labeled 10 points on the grid to the right.

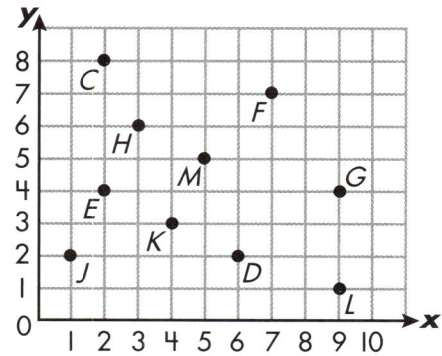

Helpful Hint

Points on a grid are located based on their (x, y) coordinates. The horizontal number is x and the vertical number is y. Point A on the grid below is at (5, 2) which is 5 to the right and 2 up from the origin. Point B is at (8, 4).

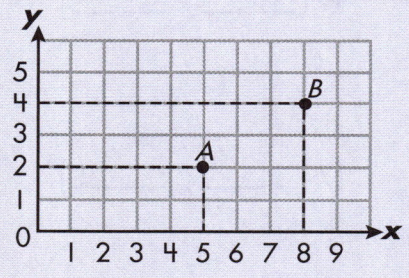

1. Which point did Lee graph at (6, 2)?

_____

2. Which point did Lee graph at (4, 3)?

_____

Spectrum Geometry
Grade 5

Chapter 7
The Coordinate Plane

NAME _____

SCORE ___/3

Plotting Ordered Pairs

Use the grid on page 72 to answer numbers 3 and 4.

3. Find the ordered pair for point M.

_____

4. Find the ordered pair for point G.

_____

5. Lee wants to plot point A on his grid at (5, 1). Plot this point on the grid below.

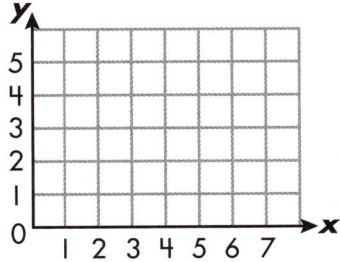

Spectrum Geometry
Grade 5

Chapter 7
The Coordinate Plane

73

NAME _____

SCORE ◯ /2

Ordered Pairs on a Coordinate Plane

Read the problem carefully and solve. Show your work under each question.

Sarah decides to show the location of some places in her neighborhood using a grid. She locates these places by plotting and labeling the points on the grid.

Use the grid below to answer each question.

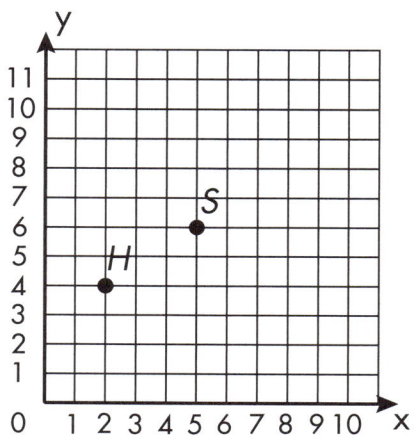

1. Sarah plots her house on the grid. She labels the point *H*. What ordered pair represents point *H*?

   _____

2. Sarah also plots her school on the grid. She labels the point *S*. What ordered pair represents point *S*?

   _____

NAME _____

SCORE ☐ / 2

Ordered Pairs on a Coordinate Plane

Use the grid below to answer each question.

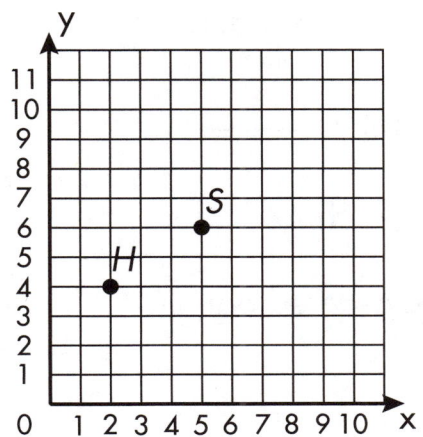

3. Sarah wants to plot her friend Lisa's house at (3, 10) on the grid. She plans to label the point *L*. Plot the ordered pair (3, 10) on the grid above and label the point *L*.

4. Sarah loves to take her dog to the park. She plots the park on her grid at (9, 1), and labels the point *P*. Plot the ordered pair (9, 1) on the grid and label the point *P*.

Spectrum Geometry
Grade 5

Chapter 7
The Coordinate Plane
75

NAME _____

Check What You Learned

The Coordinate Plane

Use the grid to name a point for each ordered pair.

1. (10, 5) _____   (1, 1) _____

2. (4, 9) _____   (7, 4) _____

Using the same grid, name the ordered pair for each point.

3. B (_____ , _____)   G (_____ , _____)

4. E (_____ , _____)   A (_____ , _____)

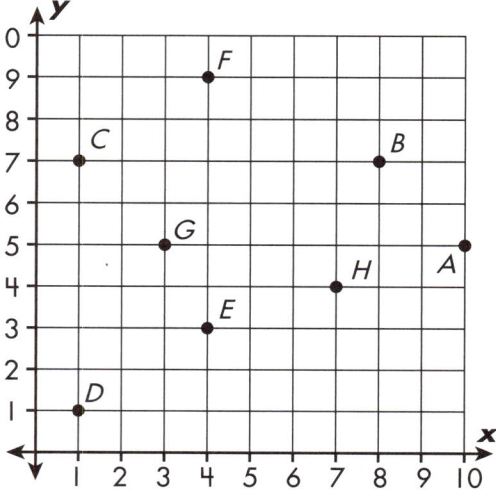

Plot the points shown on the grid. Label the points.

5. M (3, 4)   N (9, 6)
6. O (5, 7)   P (7, 8)
7. Q (7, 2)   R (8, 7)

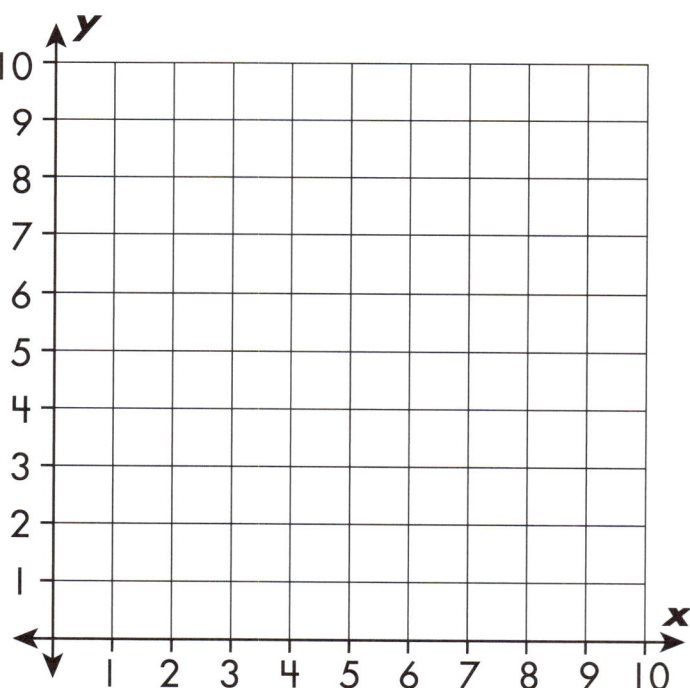

Final Test Chapters 1–7

NAME _____

Match each figure to its name.

1. ray _____
2. perpendicular lines _____
3. acute angle _____
4. parallel lines _____
5. line _____
6. obtuse angle _____
7. line segment _____
8. point _____
9. right angle _____
10. intersecting lines _____

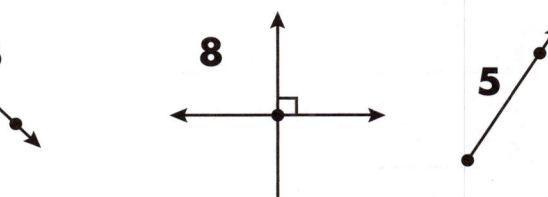
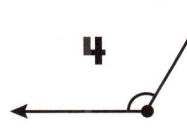
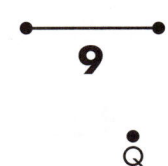
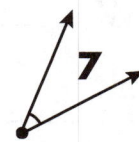
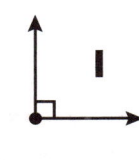
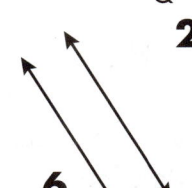
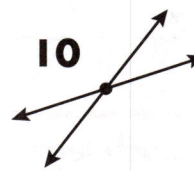

Find the area of each rectangle.

    a   **b**

11. 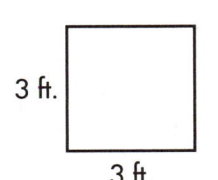 square (3 ft. × 3 ft.)   rectangle $2\frac{2}{5}$ yd. × $8\frac{4}{5}$ yd.

_____ square feet   _____ square yards

Find the volume of each rectangular solid.

12. 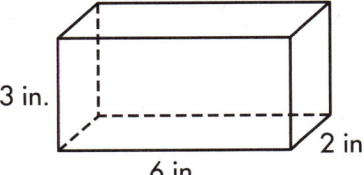 (3 in. × 6 in. × 2 in.)   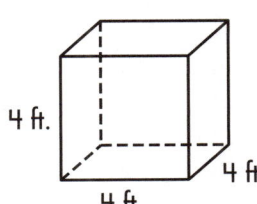 (4 ft. × 4 ft. × 4 ft.)

_____ cubic inches   _____ cubic feet

Spectrum Geometry
Grade 5

Final Test Chapters 1–7

Use the grid to find the ordered pair for each labeled point.

	a	b
13.	B _____	V _____
14.	S _____	A _____
15.	W _____	N _____
16.	T _____	R _____
17.	Z _____	P _____

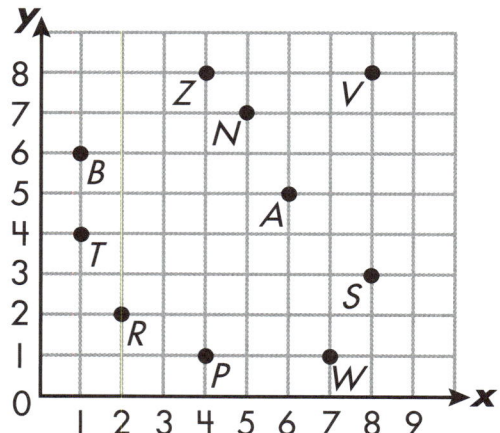

Match each term with its picture. You may use a letter more than once. A question may have more than one answer.

18. trapezoid _____
19. triangular pyramid _____
20. rhombus _____
21. cone _____
22. kite _____
23. cylinder _____
24. square _____
25. cube _____
26. rectangle _____
27. triangular solid _____

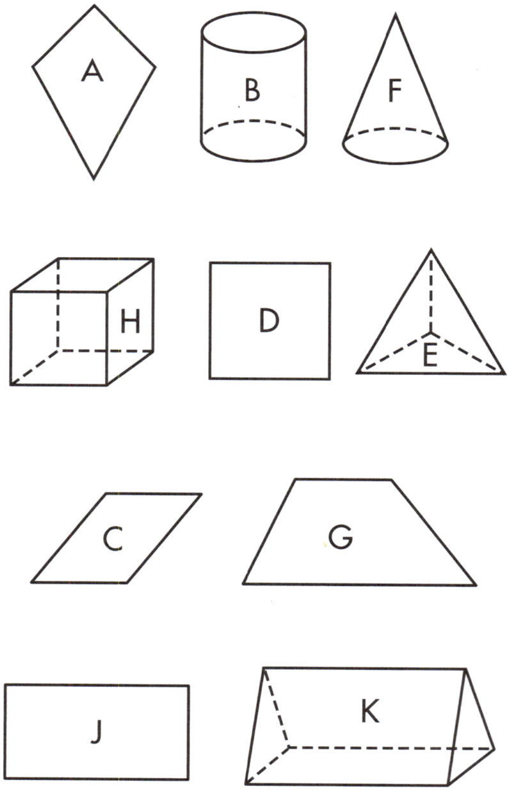

Final Test Chapters 1–7

Use a protractor to measure the following angles.

28.

a 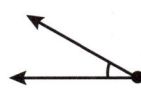 _____ degrees

b  _____ degrees

---

Find the area of each rectangle.

29.

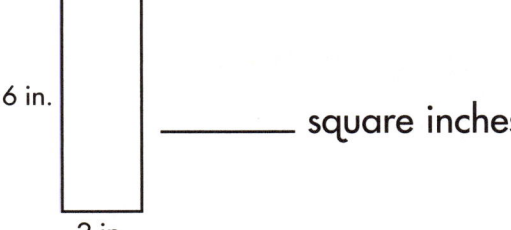 _____ square inches

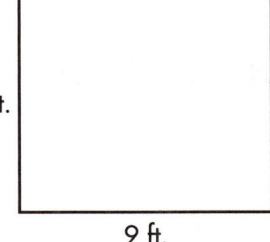 _____ square feet

---

Find the volume of each rectangular solid.

30.

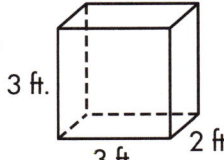 _____ cubic feet

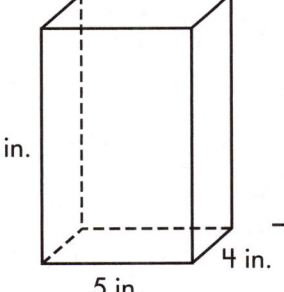 _____ cubic inches

NAME _____

Final Test Chapters 1–7

Read the problem carefully and solve. Show your work under each question.

The Big View Land Survey Company takes high altitude photos of land. The company uses the photos to make land measurements. Various groups use the photos for plans to develop or maintain the land.

---

31. A worker marks a photo that looks like the one shown below. What is the figure called?

 _____

32. The edges of a field make an angle like the one shown below. What kind of angle is it?

 _____

33. On a photo, the roof of a building has the shape shown below. What is the name of this shape?

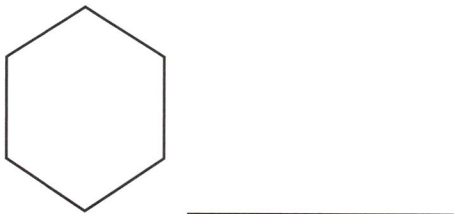

_____

34. From a photo, an analyst finds the dimensions of a building. What is the volume of the building?

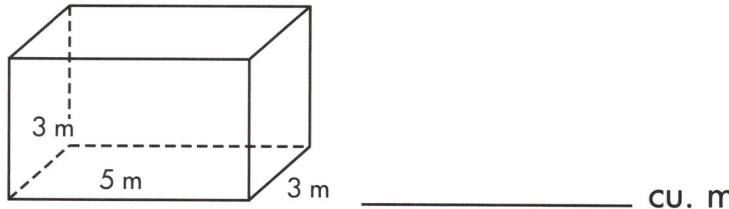 _____ cu. m

Spectrum Geometry
Grade 5

Final Test Chapters 1–7

Solve each problem. Show your work under each question.

35. Mr. Peate is building a rectangular fence around his house. The fence will be 32 feet long and 29 feet wide. What will be the perimeter of the fence?

The perimeter will be _____ feet.

36. Sherman developed a photo 4 inches wide by 6 inches in length. What is the area of the photograph?

The photo is _____ square inches.

37. The Williams family bought a house 4,560 square feet in area. The house is 60 feet long. How wide is the house?

The house is _____ feet wide.

38. Ms. Ferris owns a barn 12 yards long, 9 yards high, and 11 yards wide. If Ms. Ferris's barn is rectangular, what is the volume of her barn?

The volume of her barn is _____ cubic yards.

Spectrum Geometry
Grade 5

Final Test Chapters 1–7

Solve each problem. Show your work under each question.

39. A soccer field is an example of a rectangle. If a soccer field is 90 meters long and 45 meters wide, what is the perimeter of the soccer field?

The perimeter of the field is _____ meters.

40. Julie is cutting out triangle pieces for her scrapbook. The sides of the triangle are 3 centimeters by 4 centimeters by 2 centimeters. What is the perimeter of the triangle?

The perimeter of the triangle is _____ centimeters.

41. Lea wants to put carpet on her bedroom floor. Her bedroom is 4 meters long and 6 meters wide. How much carpet does Lea need to cover the floor?

Lea needs _____ square meters of carpet.

42. A swimming pool is 3 meters in depth, 8 meters in length, and 6 meters in width. What is the volume of the swimming pool?

The volume of the swimming pool is _____ cubic meters.

Spectrum Geometry
Grade 5

Scoring Record for Pretests, Posttests, Mid-Test, and Final Test

NAME _____

Pretests, Posttests, Mid-Test, and Final Test	Your Score	Performance			
		Excellent	Very Good	Fair	Needs Improvement
Chapter 1 Pretest	___ of 16	15–16	13–14	10–12	9 or fewer
Chapter 1 Posttest	___ of 16	15–16	13–14	10–12	9 or fewer
Chapter 2 Pretest	___ of 6	6	5	4	3 or fewer
Chapter 2 Posttest	___ of 5	5	4	3	2 or fewer
Chapter 3 Pretest	___ of 10	9–10	8–9	6–7	5 or fewer
Chapter 3 Posttest	___ of 15	14–15	12–13	9–11	8 or fewer
Chapter 4 Pretest	___ of 4	4	3	2	1
Chapter 4 Posttest	___ of 6	6	5	4	3 or fewer
Chapter 5 Pretest	___ of 9	8–9	7–8	6–7	5 or fewer
Chapter 5 Posttest	___ of 12	11–12	10–11	8–9	7 or fewer
Chapter 6 Pretest	___ of 4	4	3	2	1
Chapter 6 Posttest	___ of 5	5	4	3	2 or fewer
Chapter 7 Pretest	___ of 18	17–18	15–16	11–14	10 or fewer
Chapter 7 Posttest	___ of 18	17–18	15–16	11–14	10 or fewer
Mid-Test	___ of 33	32–33	27–31	20–26	19 or fewer
Final Test	___ of 62	59–62	50–58	38–49	37 or fewer

Spectrum Geometry
Grade 5

Scoring Record

Answer Key

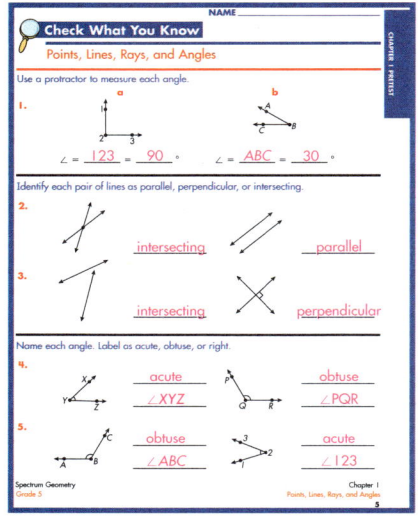

5

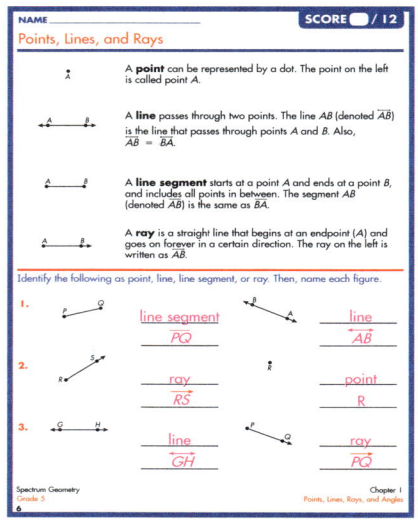

6

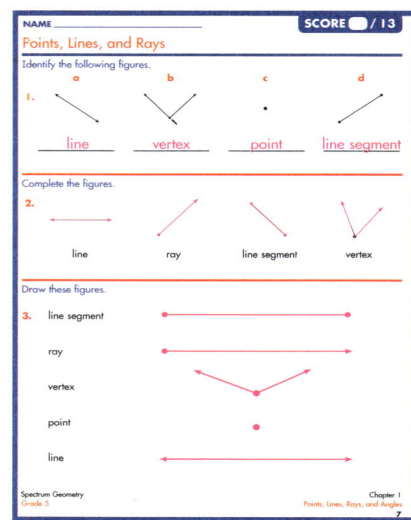

7

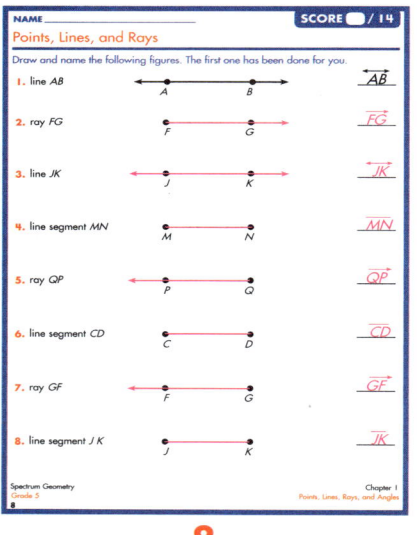

8

9

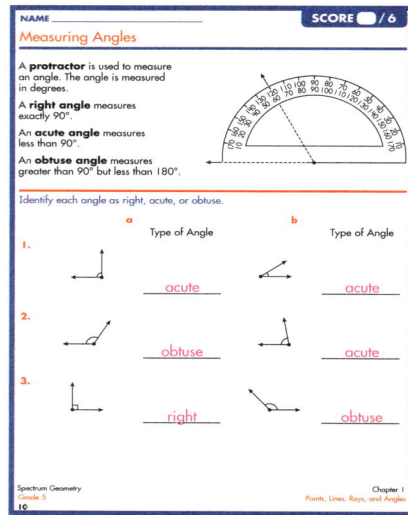

10

Spectrum Geometry
Grade 5

84

Answer Key

Answer Key

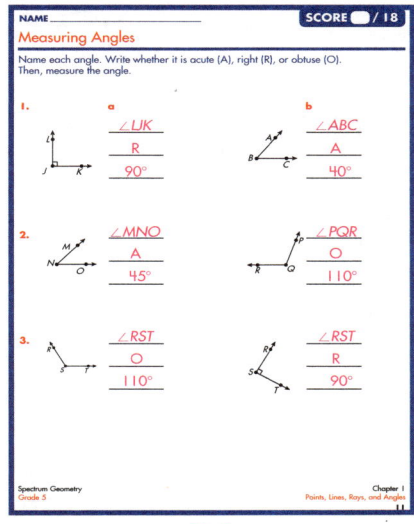
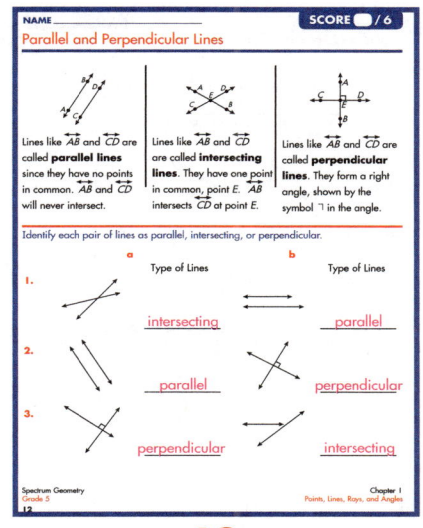
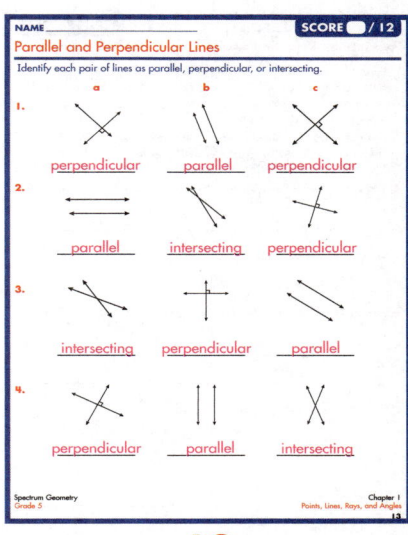

Spectrum Geometry
Grade 5

Answer Key

85

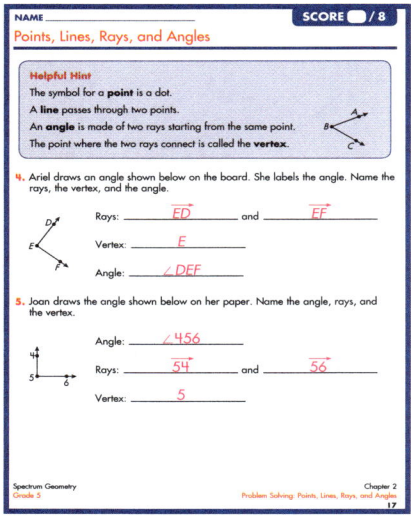

Answer Key

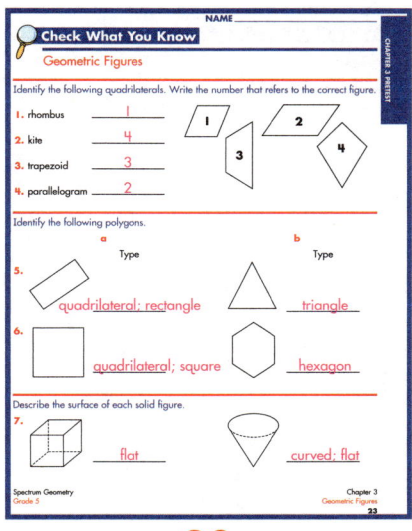
23

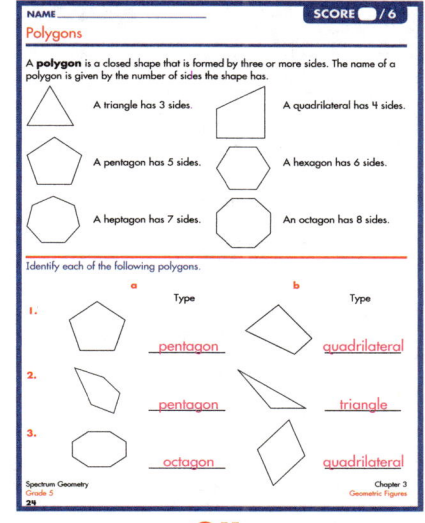
24

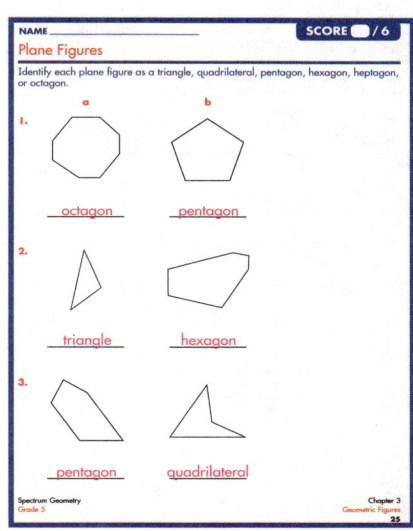
25

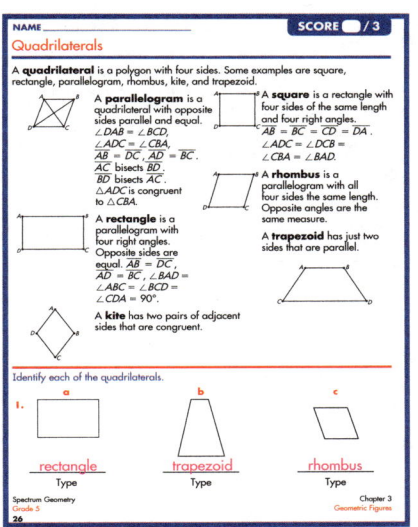
26

27

28

Answer Key

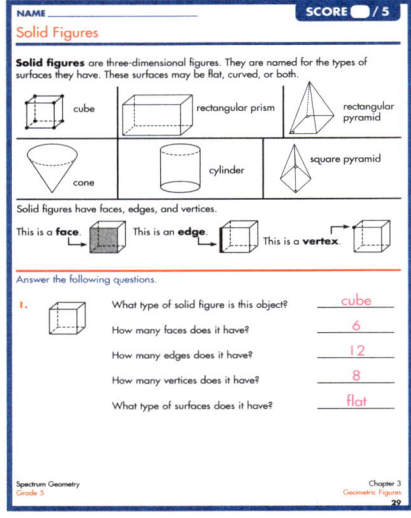
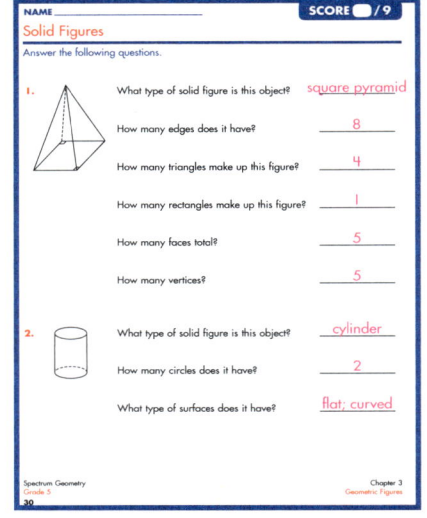
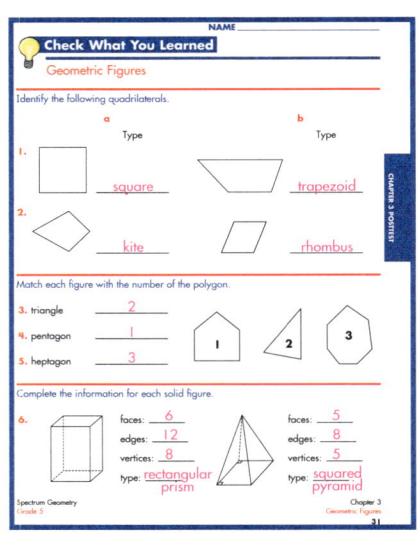

Spectrum Geometry
Grade 5

Answer Key

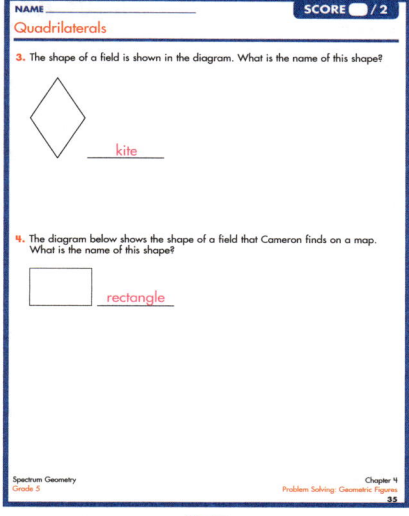

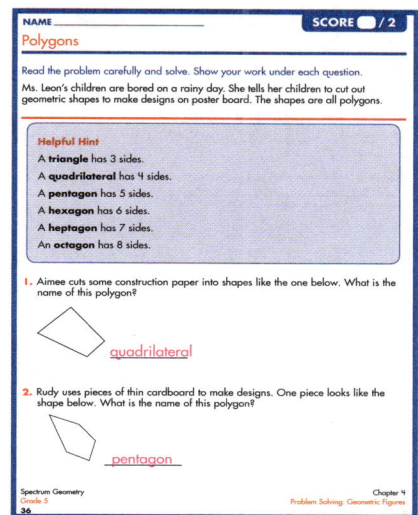

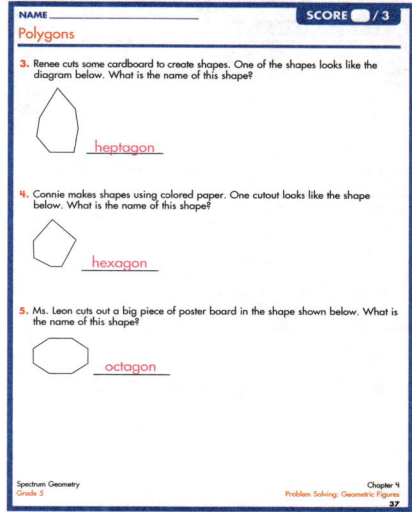

Spectrum Geometry
Grade 5

Answer Key

89

Answer Key

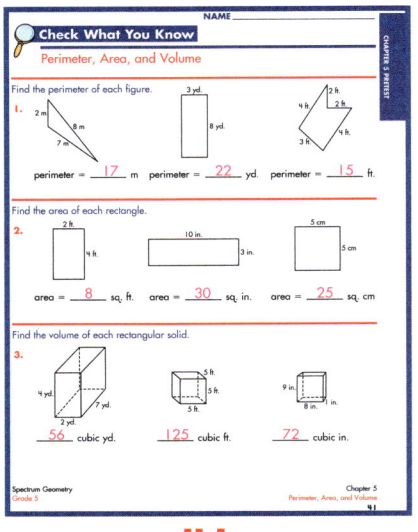
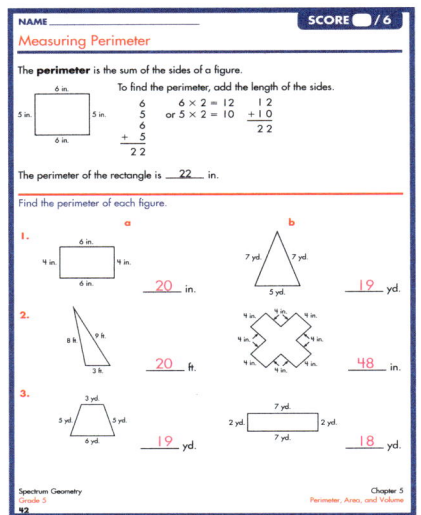
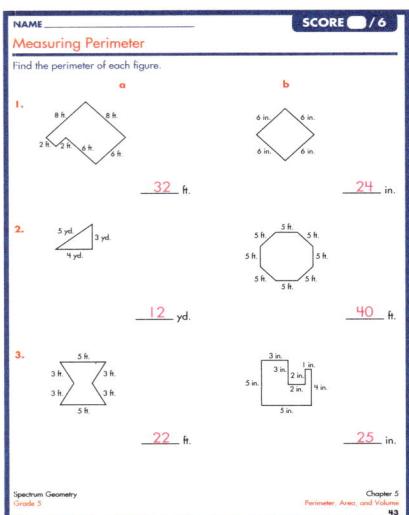

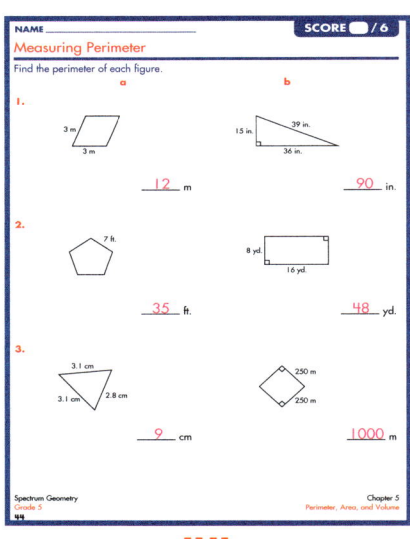
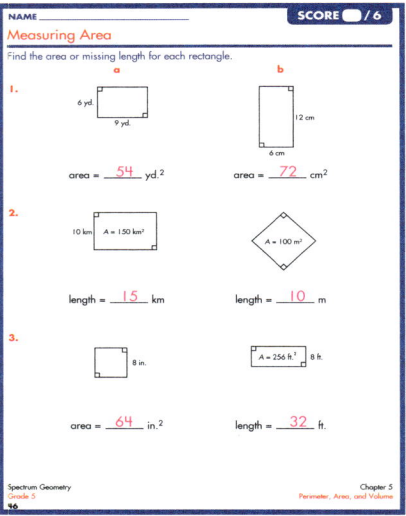

Spectrum Geometry
Grade 5

Answer Key

90

Answer Key

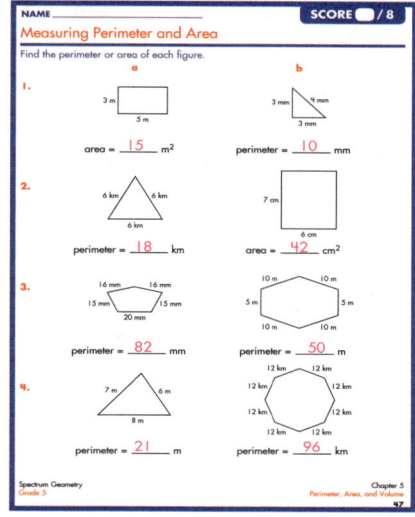

47

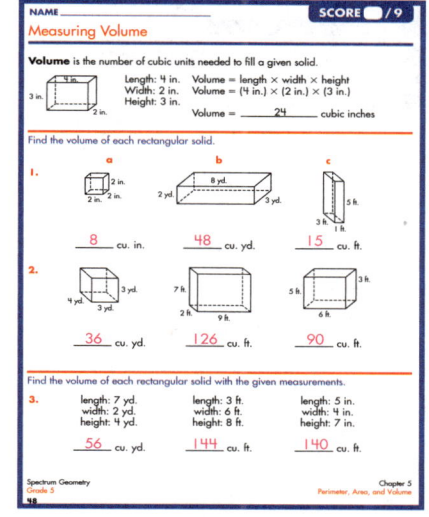

48

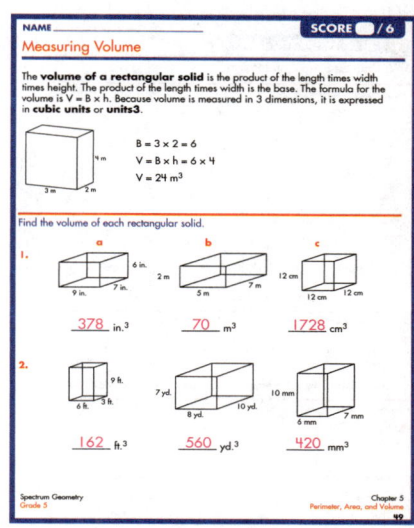

49

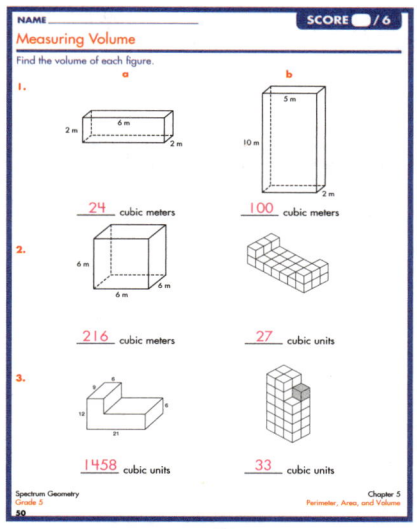

50

51

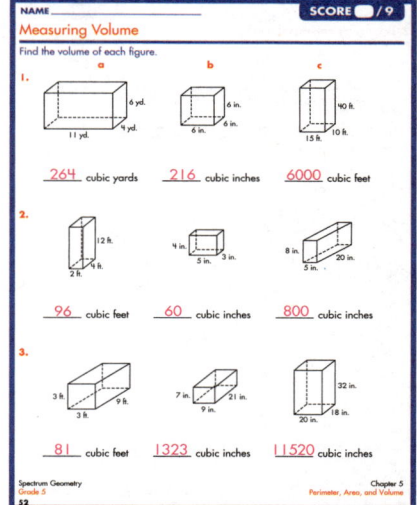

52

Answer Key

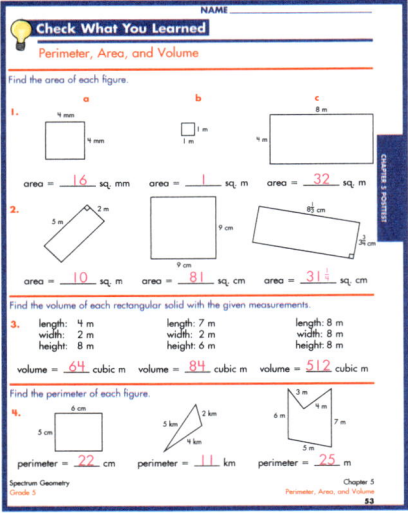
53

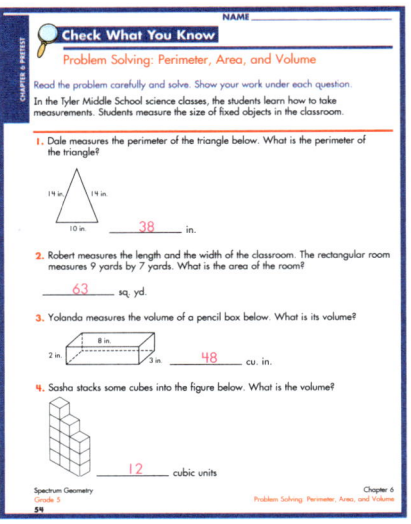
54

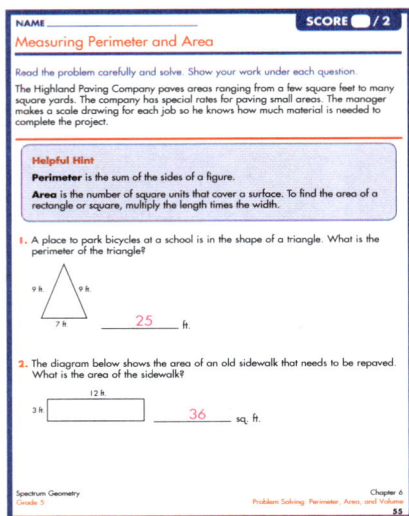
55

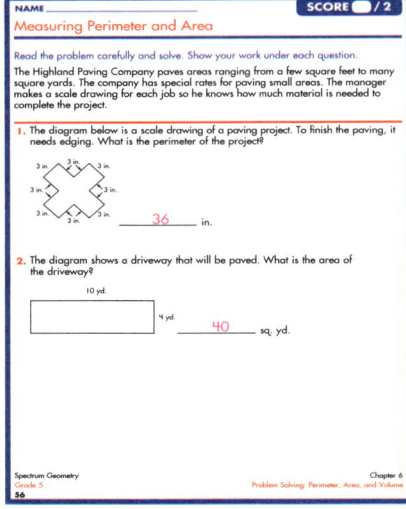
56

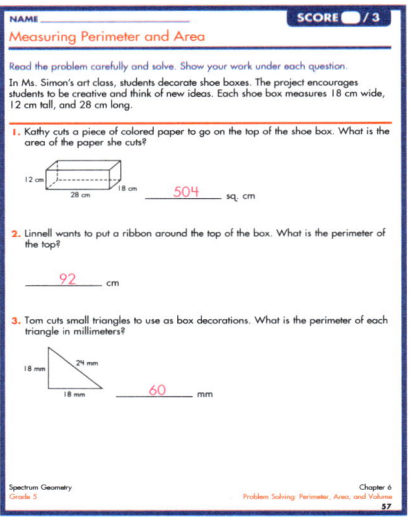
57

58

Answer Key

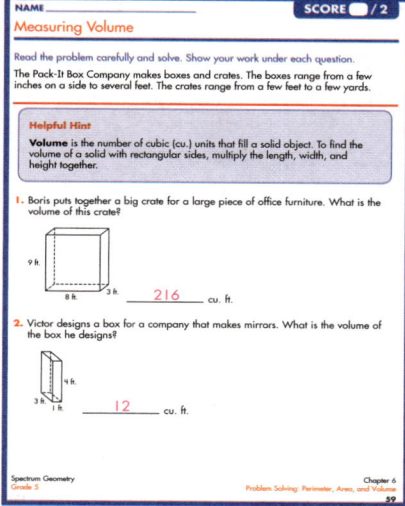
59

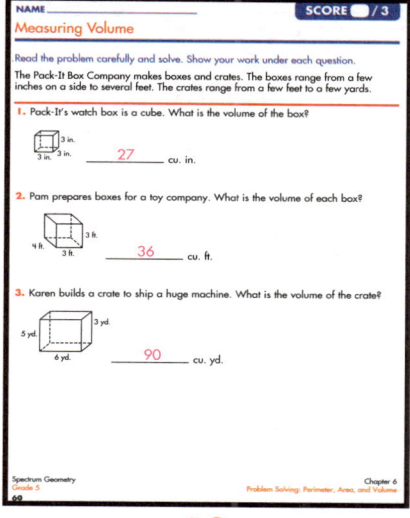
60

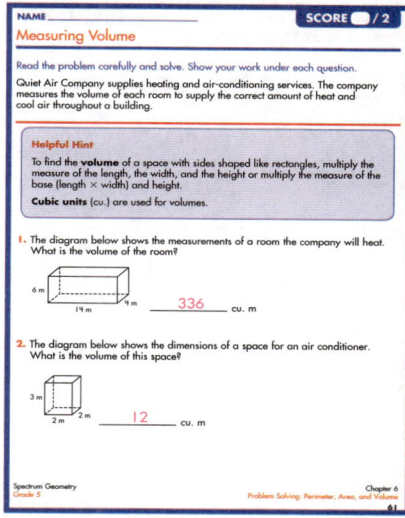
61

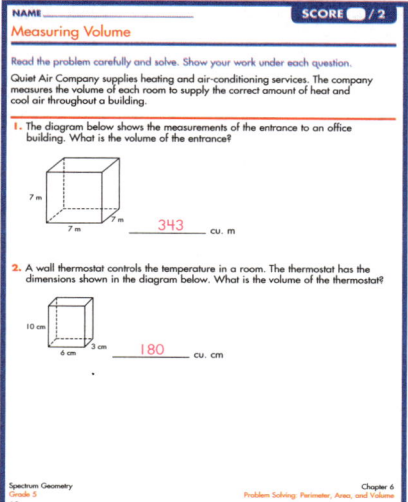
62

63

64

Spectrum Geometry
Grade 5

Answer Key

Answer Key

Page 65
Ordered Pairs on a Coordinate Plane

Identify the ordered pair from each grid.
1. a. (3, 3) b. (8, 2)

Page 66
Ordered Pairs on a Coordinate Plane

Plot each ordered pair.
1. (3, 2)
2. (2, 3)
3. (5, 5)

Page 67
Plotting Ordered Pairs

Use the grid to name the point for each ordered pair.
1. (1, 2) J   (2, 4) E
2. (3, 6) H   (9, 4) G
3. (9, 1) L   (5, 5) M
4. (2, 8) C   (4, 3) K
5. (7, 7) F   (6, 2) D

Page 68
Plotting Ordered Pairs

Use the grid to name the point for each ordered pair.
1. (7, 2) H   (3, 4) E
2. (3, 6) D   (9, 6) G
3. L(9, 5)   C(3, 3)
4. J(1, 8)   I(5, 3)
5. F(8, 8)   K(7, 4)

Page 69
Plotting Ordered Pairs

Plot each ordered pair on the grid.
1. A(1, 5)   B(5, 3)
2. C(7, 4)   D(2, 2)
3. E(4, 7)   F(9, 1)
4. G(8, 2)   H(7, 6)
5. I(6, 5)   J(1, 7)

Page 70
Plotting Ordered Pairs

Plot each ordered pair on the grid.
1. A(4, 5)   B(8, 4)
2. C(2, 3)   D(2, 2)
3. E(7, 1)   F(7, 8)
4. G(6, 4)   H(8, 3)
5. I(1, 1)   J(4, 7)

Answer Key

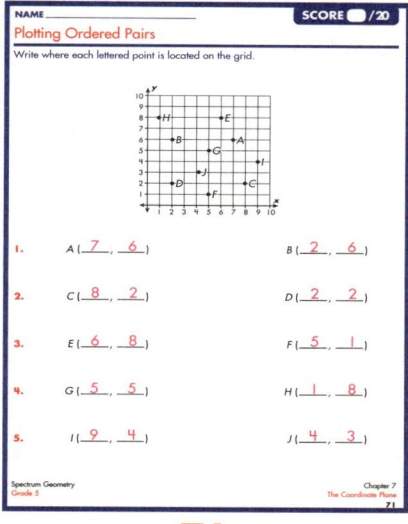

71

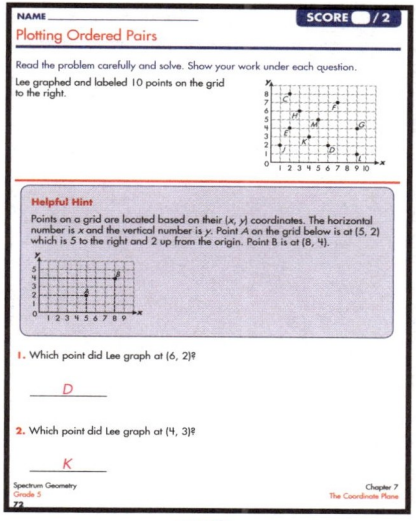

72

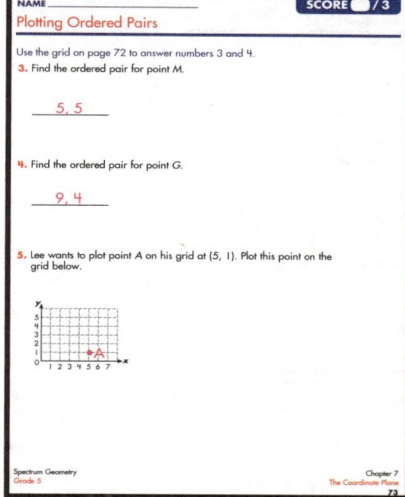

73

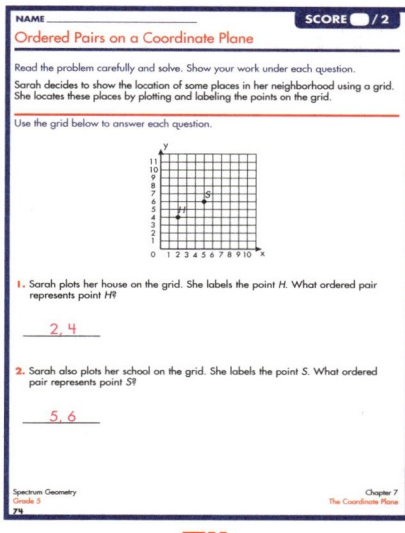

74

75

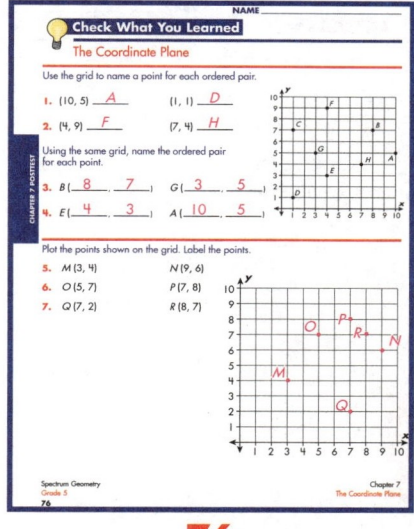

76

Spectrum Geometry
Grade 5

Answer Key

95

Answer Key

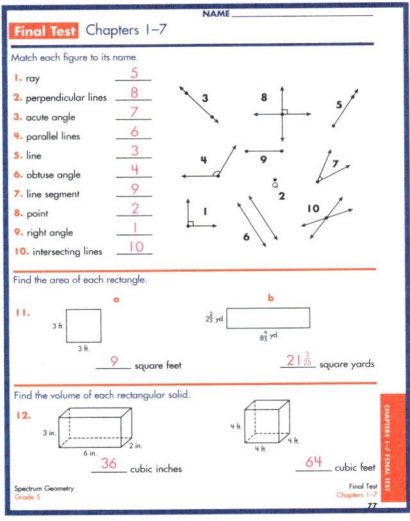

Spectrum Geometry
Grade 5